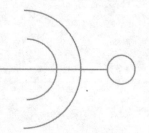

PRAISE FOR
STAR WARS JESUS

"Caleb Grimes has produced a sort of Christian commentary, poignantly and lovingly composed, to the *Star Wars* saga. There is a graceful, gentle tone to the book, which captures the pathos and child-like spirit of the movies and the myth. This is a sweet book —for fans and also for all hopers in the triumph of love."

> Paul F.M. Zahl,
> Dean/President Trinity Episcopal School
> for Ministry, Ambridge, PA

"Clearly driven by a love of both *Star Wars* and Jesus, the author works to do justice to both. The result is not what you are expecting. This extended interpretation of the six films will get you thinking about them—and your understanding of Jesus—in a fresh way. It might even help redeem Episodes I-III."

> Peter Edman,
> Editor, Metaphilm.com

"An exegesis on *Star Wars* at its finest! Caleb has managed to cleverly bridge the dichotomy between sacred and sci-fi, faith and force. This book will bring revelation to you as you explore Jesus principles through Jedi perspectives. May His Spirit be with you!"

> Glenn Lim,
> Youth Counselor and Ambassador—
> Singapore, Youth Pastor—
> Church Of Our Saviour, Singapore,
> www.glennlim.net

D0968102

STAR WARS™
JESUS

STAR WARS™
JESUS

A SPIRITUAL COMMENTARY ON THE REALITY OF THE FORCE

Caleb Grimes

WINEPRESS WP PUBLISHING

© 2007 by Caleb Grimes. All rights reserved

WinePress Publishing (PO Box 428, Enumclaw, WA 98022) functions only as book publisher. As such, the ultimate design, content, editorial accuracy, and views expressed or implied in this work are those of the author.

No part of this publication may be reproduced, stored in a retrieval system or transmitted in any way by any means—electronic, mechanical, photocopy, recording or otherwise—without the prior permission of the copyright holder, except as provided by USA copyright law.

Neither this book nor its contents are endorsed or approved by or affiliated in any way with George Lucas or Lucasfilm Ltd. The opinions contained herein are those of the author only. Star Wars is a trademark of Lucasfilm Ltd. All rights reserved.

Unless otherwise noted, all Scriptures are taken from the Holy Bible, New International Version, Copyright © 1973, 1978, 1984 by the International Bible Society. Used by permission of Zondervan Publishing House. The "NIV" and "New International Version" trademarks are registered in the United States Patent and Trademark Office by International Bible Society.

ISBN 1-57921-884-9
Library of Congress Catalog Card Number: 2006935682

Printed in Colombia.

To LLL, my lovely lady Leslie

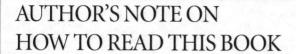

AUTHOR'S NOTE ON
HOW TO READ THIS BOOK

Readers might well tackle this book in random spurts, jumping all around as they find entries of interest, or in the traditional manner, reading from front to back. Either way works.

The 101 commentaries are chronological by movie release date and chronological within each movie. The names of each movie form the book's larger sections, while individual entries move sequentially through each film. For example, let us imagine that you, like me, are primarily interested in reading about Luke Skywalker's experiences on Dagobah. Turn to the Table of Contents, scan down to the section marked *Episode V: The Empire Strikes Back*, and find any entries containing the word *Dagobah*. The title of each entry includes the portion of each film that is under discussion, along with a short description of a specific topic.

So look down the table of contents to find something that interests you, read an entry or two, and then put it back on the coffee table. You might even want to check that topic off in the table of contents to remind yourself that you've read it.

Of course, if you choose to go from the front of the book to the back, you will find a blossoming of ideas and theories that progresses with our having learned about the Force and the Jedi with each movie's release date, spanning from 1977 to 2005.

TABLE OF CONTENTS

Episode V: The Empire Strikes Back

Episode VI: Return of the Jedi

Episode I: The Phantom Menace

Episode II: Attack of the Clones

Episode III: Revenge of the Sith

ACKNOWLEDGMENTS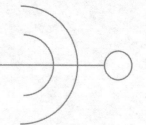

To the Holy Creator, thank you for the worlds you have made. Mere words can only attempt to thank you for all you are. To George Lucas, thank you for creating the *Star Wars* universe; your work has blessed me. To Leslie and Sam, thank you for loving *Star Wars* with me, and for encouraging me to write this book. To WinePress, thank you for publishing this book. To George Winship, thank you for your love of Star Wars and your editorial expertise.

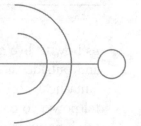

INTRODUCTION

For many of us, watching *Star Wars* is like attending Sunday school. George Lucas is often quoted as saying that he wants *Star Wars* to give a moral grounding to those of us who grow up without a strong family bond and in front of the television, an influence that Lucas sees as amoral.

Star Wars does inform our morality—our perspective on life—and, for many of us, these movies contain the images and metaphors that we look to as we go through tough times. For example, when those of us who enjoy *Star Wars* become angry, we often remember the scene in *Episode V: The Empire Strikes Back* when Yoda says, "Anger, fear, aggression—these are paths to the dark side." We think of this scene before we ever think of Jesus saying, "My peace I give to you," or "Love your enemies." Then, in our heads, we hear Luke Skywalker respond, "But how will I know the dark side from the light?" We find ourselves asking the question with him because anger and vengeance seem perfectly justified when these emotions strike us. Once again, we hear Yoda's answer, "When you are calm, at peace." As a result, we actually decide not to do certain things until we are calm or at peace.

This probably upsets some religious leaders, but it is the truth, and there it is. It is not un-Christian to handle anger this way, but it is post-Christian in the sense that individuals in the western world no longer come from a distinctly Christian background. George Lucas was one of the first filmmakers to understand the void of moral teaching that this situation creates, and he did something about it. Therefore, *Star Wars* is a mythical fairy tale that teaches many of us right from wrong, good from evil, just like Sunday school.

Of course, we love all the exciting adventures, the new worlds, and the fantastic gadgets with which these films entertain us. However, the core reason why many of us keep watching *Star Wars* so many times over has to do with the power of myth. The films teach us how to live and act, especially if we grew up in a broken home and outside the influence of a church. A myth story is typically a fantastical story about a hero who learns about and uses supernatural power to conquer problems. Through this vehicle, myths often teach natural and social truths. In this sense, religions—or systems of belief—are also myths. They also deal with the supernatural in a fantastical way to tell us how to live in the natural and social world. In addition, there is often a hero in our religions. Because we pursue truth through myth, there are deep sociological and psychological connections we all have between myths and our own lives. This explanation of myth, however, is very cold to the extent that myths and religions are also very much about joy and imagination. If we find something to be true, a natural response is celebration, both inward and outward. As you might well imagine from the title, this book is a celebration of the beautiful commonalities between *Star Wars,* the most popular myth of our time, and Jesus, the real live myth of all time.

Even George Lucas might have underestimated how necessary is his myth. *Star Wars* has become so popular in the last 30 years that many have taken the philosophy behind *Star Wars* much more seriously than Lucas ever intended, to a point that some even call the Jedi religion their own. This stems in part from the post-Christian nature of the world in which we live, but also from a great love for this series, as well as the fascinating ideas and worlds it presents. From interviews and statements quoting George Lucas, however, it is clear that he never intended the ideas within this series to be its own belief system. In fact, if taken as a belief system in and of itself, the philosophy behind *Star Wars* fails. This does not prevent us, however, from looking for those places where the Force might be real in our lives. For this reason, it is my purpose here to show where Jesus is already present in the *Star Wars* films. As such, this book seeks to say yes to everything in *Star Wars* that resonates with the person of Jesus, before it clarifies where the two diverge and points out the gaps that remain in our interpretation of the Force as it applies to our own world.

I would like to also be clear on another point. It is not my goal to convert to Christianity those who love *Star Wars*.

What is so much like Jesus about the Force, "an energy field that surrounds us and penetrates us and binds the galaxy together"? How can good and evil both be part of the same Force if it is supposed to be like Jesus? You may ask, "If the Force is real, why can't I levitate that orange on the table and make it float over to me on the couch? I've been trying all day long." Can Jesus help me sense a disturbance in the Force? Does Jesus show up in *Star Wars* somewhere? Read on and find out.

Caleb Grimes

P.S.—To the five people who have not yet seen the *Star Wars* movies, this book contains plot spoilers. :)

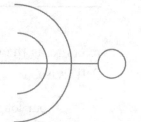

EPISODE IV
A NEW HOPE

[1] LUKE ON THE MOUND—SEHNSUCHT.

Perhaps the most indelible scene in all of cinematic history is seeing Luke Skywalker climb onto the dirt mound to watch the
setting of Tatooine's twin suns. We hear the longing melody of the
French horn. Luke is frustrated that his uncle is not allowing him to
submit an application to the academy. Before he goes back to clean-
ing the droids his uncle just purchased from the Jawas (C-3PO and
R2-D2), Luke puts one foot up on the berm of their sunken home
and looks out at the desert horizon and the double sunset. From this
context, we know Luke is dreaming of a better life. Is this scene only
about teenage angst?

Not even remotely! Whenever it was that we first saw this scene,
not knowing what was to come, we grieve that Luke is held back
from his dreams. Seeing the end of the movie, however, then experiencing the remaining films of the original trilogy causes us to
understand that this one quiet moment has taken on much more
significance. The work of Joseph Campbell, the preeminent scholar
of mythology in our time, heavily influenced George Lucas, especially during the making of *Star Wars*. Campbell writes,

> ". . . mythology is the penultimate truth—penultimate because the
> ultimate cannot be put into words . . . It is important to live life
> with the experience—and therefore the knowledge—of its mys-
> tery and of your own mystery. This gives life a new radiance, a
> new harmony, a new splendor."[1]
>
> (The Power of Myth, p. 206)

Luke is sensing the mystery of his future, wanting there to be
something more. This scene contains that feeling that C.S. Lewis

refers to as the German word *Sehnsucht*, which Lewis identifies as part of Joy.

> ". . . our longing to be reunited with something in the universe from which we now feel cut off, to be on the inside of some door which we have always seen from the outside, is no mere neurotic fancy, but the truest index of our real situation. And to be at last summoned inside would be both glory and honor beyond all our merits and also the healing of that old ache."[2]
>
> (*The Weight of Glory*, p. 15)

In another of his works, Lewis adds,

> "Joy is distinct not only from pleasure in general but even from aesthetic pleasure. It must have the stab, the pang, the inconsolable longing."[3]
>
> (*Surprised by Joy*, p. 78)

Luke Skywalker aches for more. He feels a tug towards something about which he knows nothing. At the same time, there is an attachment to the nature of his home planet as seen in his gazing at the double sunset of Tatooine. He did not know what to make of all the feelings, all the longing. Is this a subconscious hunger to know the Force, which is similar to our desire to know a personal God? Perhaps it even represents to us a quiet need for worship—a yearning for our home with God. Our soul, as with Luke's, is responding to our Creator's call to us.

[2] First scenes of *Star Wars*. Droids in the desert. Coincidence as an agent of the Force to bring about what is possible versus what is probable.

Stepping back in time from this book's first entry to the very first minutes ever seen of *Star Wars*, there is a space battle going on and two droids are caught in the middle of it. The Rebel's blockade runner, *Tantive IV*, is pulled in by the Star Destroyer's powerful tractor beam. Princess Leia Organa makes one final and desperate attempt to deliver the Death Star's blueprints to the Rebel Forces by sending R2-D2 to Tatooine to find Obi-Wan Kenobi and enlist his help.

Out of the coincidental happenings of the adventures of the small droid R2-D2 and his tag-along partner C-3PO, the virtually impossible destruction of an evil, oppressive, tyrannical Empire by a tiny band of bold souls is set into motion.

Star Wars begins with the barely possible story of the droids on their quest. It keeps adding and adding to the seemingly insurmountable tasks of those who serve the good side of the Force. Without intervention by the Force, R2-D2 and C-3PO probably would never have reached Obi-Wan Kenobi; Luke Skywalker would probably still be stuck on his Uncle Owen's moisture farm indefinitely; and Han Solo most likely would be captured or killed by Jabba the Hutt's henchmen.

Flannery O'Connor writes about what is possible in terms of the writer and the writing process that he goes through.

> ". . . if the writer believes that our life is and will remain essentially mysterious . . . Such a writer will be interested in what we don't understand rather than in what we do. He will be interested in possibility rather than probability."[4]
>
> (*Mystery and Manners*, p. 42)

We watch the *Star Wars* movies and we love the *Star Wars* movies because there is something in us that says, "No, they are going to make it. There is an outside chance that good will win." The improbable happening is part of the very magic of *Star Wars*—and it is a major reason why audiences love *Star Wars*. There is much more to this cinematic series than a cool new world with aliens, spaceships, gadgets, a princess, and a darkly evil bad guy. We are suckers for the story of an underdog. Indeed, what could be more "underdoggy" than two feeble droids facing an evil Empire of unsurpassed power, overwhelming technology, and unchecked authority? But we relate to these desperate odds. Most of us are underdogs too; we see ourselves and think, "If the Force can direct the path of the droids, couldn't the Force also direct our paths to make good things happen?" This possibility mysteriously rings true to us, and here is why—the possible happening in spite of the probable is what God does when he uses the smallest, the least among us, to confound the greatest. Coincidences, as we perceive them, are often the way God brings about the possible.

Was it a coincidence that Moses was found, taken, and reared by a member of the Egyptian court? Was it a coincidence that the walls of Jericho fell down? Was the life of Jesus simply a historical coincidence with the Old Testament's prophesies? Was the tearing of the curtain between the Holy of Holies and the congregation in the temple, at the moment of Christ's death, merely another such coincidence?

Humanity's witness of these personal and corporate phenomena throughout history has created archetypal patterns that exist inside of us to the point where we see these mysterious and supernatural kinds of stories as organic to our own beings. In fact, they are so ingrained in us that we often mistake them as originating from inside ourselves instead of from God's work in us. This perspective is the main difference that a believer in Christianity would have with Joseph Campbell, who was the leading authority on myth in our time, and one of the main influences on George Lucas. Campbell would say that God is a construction of the myths of the world.

Through the image of the droids in the desert, we understand the crazy impossibility of the Rebel Alliance even making a dent in the Galactic Empire. Through the seeming coincidences of the droids' adventures, like seeing the wind blow through the leaves on a tree, we understand the working of the Force.

[3] Old Ben Kenobi finds Luke in the Jundland Wastes.
How to recognize the Force
moving in your life.

The previous entry expresses how one can see the droid's coincidences in the way they find Obi-Wan Kenobi and Luke Skywalker as a movement of the Force. Entry 2 also explains how coincidences are seen as the way we perceive God working, mysteriously making the possible happen, instead of the merely probable. God and the Force are similar in that a quality of both is a mystical, unseen power that directs us if we allow him or it to do so. Recognizing this direction is a vital part of our spiritual natures, as well as that of the Jedi. In Ben Kenobi, we see a Jedi identifying and taking direction from the Force.

In subsequently released films, we learn that two decades before this scene, Obi-Wan Kenobi witnesses the fall of the Republic and the rise of the Empire. He was there when it all went wrong, when Palpatine deceived and murdered the Jedi Order, when Anakin turned to evil, when the clone army were switched from defending the Republic to being the henchmen for an evil Emperor. As one of two Jedi Knights still alive although forced into exile, Obi-Wan undoubtedly comprehended that the busy lives of the Jedi in the Republic took them away from feeling the Force. This separation diminished their power and allowed evil to creep in virtually unseen. He must also have sensed that someday there would have to be a return of the Jedi influence to the universe to fight what had become an extremely powerful and oppressive evil. During all those years, he must have wondered about the purpose of his watching over Luke on Tatooine, and asked himself and Yoda (through the Force) whether his skills wouldn't be better served somewhere else? The evil Empire is growing stronger every day, but Obi-Wan does not resort to frantic movements or panicked responses, he listens to the Force and remains still. Only in stillness can one learn to hear its voice. Only when one hears its voice can one respond.

Obi-Wan had dwelled in this desolate place, keeping an eye on Luke Skywalker since the boy's birth. Just before we see Obi-Wan in this scene, he undoubtedly felt compelled by the Force to go to the canyon in the Jundland Wastes where he eventually finds and rescues Luke. This was the Force directing him. Finding Luke with R2-D2, instead of R2-D2 accomplishing his mission alone, was not a meaningless coincidence. Ben senses the Force moving even further, realizing that the time for action has finally arrived. This succession of events causes Obi-Wan to sit and think in his hovel. He considers not only the plea for help from Princess Leia Organa, but also the way in which that message comes to him, and he to it.

This is like sensing an urging of the Holy Spirit in your life. Being mindful of a succession of events, or things perceived as coincidences, is a good way to listen to God and become wiser; to learn to take those paths that he is directing you to take. Ben Kenobi learned to listen to the Force during all those years in the desert. If we do this carelessly, without learning how to listen to God, we become superstitious about random events and false signs. The right way is to learn to recognize the Holy Spirit moving in a similar way to how *Star Wars* depicts the Force moving; like Obi-Wan after all these years suddenly confronted with Luke Skywalker and the droids and the ultimate mission. Christian circles tend to call it looking for an open door or being led. In baseball, it is called waiting for your pitch. In Taoism, it is called Acceptance. (Note this is not the time to get into the shortcomings of these various concepts, just to compare similar, if not exact, ideas with each other.) The important thing is to realize a living Force trying to help and direct your life.

[4] THE JEDI CONCEPT OF TIME.

Ben Kenobi is so awesome. Here is how he reacts to being guided into action by the Force: He ponders Princess Leia's hologram message, turns to Luke and says, "You must learn the ways of the Force if you're to come with me to Alderaan." Ha! The fact that Luke is present with him in his abode after all the years does not seem to surprise Ben Kenobi, and that Luke will go with him to Alderaan is a foregone conclusion! His immediate thought seems to be, "The time to train you has arrived, of course." Ben's wisdom in recognizing the moving of the Force and the way in which he selflessly responds is a wonderful example of time being nothing and everything to a Jedi.

Ben and Yoda have each had years of isolation prior to the start of Luke's training. The pace of life, whether fast or painfully slow, does not seem to be an issue. A Jedi is centered in a different sense of the passage of time. When a Jedi asks, "What time is it?" he does not mean the hour of the clock. Instead, the question is, "has the fullness of time come for a certain thing to happen?" It is a good practice for us to ask, "What time is it?" in a similar quest for wisdom. The result is that we are able to start living according to the leading of the Holy Spirit. We do not spend time with someone until the clock says it is time for us to go, but rather we spend the necessary time with every person that we need to spend. Within this context, love, communication, and relationships are more important than getting to the next place we are going in life. We focus instead on what it is we are to give to this person, or say to this person, or be to this person, and what they are to give or say or be to us. This is a major way that God leads us and works in us. If we go strictly by the clock—think following the letter of the law—it is possible to miss what God is trying to say to us and do in us and be in us. Relationships with others are just one application. The Jedi seem to do all things with this view of time. Living in this way is to discover the purpose of time.

Throughout the Bible we read about the idea of a fullness of time. The time came when the world was so wicked that God had to flood it out, and the time came for the Israelites to take the land that was promised them. Jesus came to us in the fullness of time for him to come, and he is coming back in the fullness of time. The time for something to happen is not bound by a clock. Perhaps one of the reasons why God tells us we won't know when Jesus will come back is that the fullness of time does not work like a clock, so the concept of *when* is more fluid than a simple counting of seconds. Therefore, the answer to when Christ is coming back is not a matter of counting time, but rather of counting the fullness of God's prophesies and the work that we are to do as his people. We are involved in the making and the determining of this kind of time. Ben recognizes the fullness of time has come for Luke Skywalker to become a Jedi, and for himself to come out of exile. This, then, is a true metaphor for how God works in us.

Ecclesiastes, in the third chapter, teaches that there is a season for everything in order to show us that, paradoxically, there is order to life along with the meaninglessness. Then, in the eighth chapter, it states that the wise man knows the proper time and procedure for every matter, just as Obi-Wan senses in his own situation. When we ask ourselves, "What time is it?" part of the wisdom in knowing the answer is having a selfless motivation. Ben has this, then seems to ask himself, "What is the next thing that needs to be done?" In this way, Ben listens to the Force, and what he does or does not do is based on this concept of time.

[5] "You must do what you feel is right, of course."

Luke   —   "Alderaan? I'm not going to Alderaan. I've got to go home. It's late, I'm in for it as it is."

Ben   —   "I need your help, Luke. I'm getting too old for this sort of thing. She needs your help."

Luke   —   "I can't get involved! I've got work to do! It's not that I like the Empire. I hate it! But there's nothing I can do about it right now. It's such a long way from here."

Ben   —   "That's your uncle talking."

Luke   —   "My uncle. How am I ever going to explain this?"

Ben   —   "Learn about the Force, Luke."

Luke   —   "Look, I can take you as far as Anchorhead. You can get a transport there to Mos Eisley or wherever you're going."

Ben   —   "You must do what you feel is right, of course."

Episode IV: A New Hope

Not that the Bible exists in Luke's world, but he is trying to respect and honor his parents, which is the fifth Commandment—Exodus 20. Likewise, Ben is presenting the idea that becoming a Jedi and fighting the Empire are more right than obeying Luke's Uncle Owen, which is similar to becoming Jesus' disciple and comparatively hating our mother and father and even ourselves for the sake of following him (Luke 14:26).

Which is right for Luke to do? On a larger scale, where is the line between submitting to our governing authorities (Romans 13:1) and obeying everything Christ has commanded us (Matthew 28:20) when the two are at odds? Sure there are huge issues on which we easily agree, such as fighting a dictator. However, what happens when we confront the more subtle issues? There is no nice-like-a-cliché answer for those types of situations. If we love our parents, or our government, or our society, or anything more than God, we are wrong. Also, doing or thinking something God does not want us to do or think is wrong. Not following God's lead could be very wrong.

Figuring out where, when, and how we need to follow God, though, especially when it goes against the teachings of our parents or leaders, is the process of developing the masculine part of our identities, and it is a large part of becoming an adult. (For more discussion on the masculine and feminine side of ourselves, see entry 37.) There is no guarantee our parents will understand. There is no guarantee something emotionally or physically violent will not happen to us. Many people have been tortured and martyred in this pursuit. The only thing that we can be sure of is that we have to make the decision ourselves. Our parents are not always wrong and we are not always right. It comes down to this, to quote Ben's response to Luke, "You must do what you feel is right, of course."

The problem is that what feels right to us is often wrong. "There is a way that seems right to a man, but in the end it leads to death" (Proverbs 14:12). Luke Skywalker was acting immaturely here because he was still a young teenager. He lacked the awesome peace and calmness that experience and training gave to Obi-Wan Kenobi. The reason why education and training—especially in the spiritual realm—are so important is so we can become a Ben Kenobi instead of remaining stuck in our thinking as was young Luke, or worse, as was Uncle Owen. Education and training are also vital because important decisions that become milestones in our lives often test us. And very frequently, we must make these decisions alone, often in split seconds. In those moments, we must act instinctively to do what we feel is right. It was not fair that Luke Skywalker had an immediate decision to make and was not fully ready to make it. This is often how adulthood rudely comes upon us. It seems Luke knows, deep down inside, that it is the right time to go with Ben. Yet, it is not just his devotion to Uncle Owen and Aunt Beru that holds him back. Luke might be a bit scared by this sudden opportunity. In the question of "To be or not to be," Luke decides not to be, not to join Ben, and not to become a Jedi Knight like his father before him. It takes the destruction of his home and the gruesome murders of his aunt and uncle to get him off the decision making fence. It is in this manner that the reluctant Luke Skywalker, like so many mythical heroes before him, starts on his quest.

[6] REAL-LIFE DEATH STARS AND THEIR MAKERS. HOW TO IDENTIFY THEM AND WHAT TO DO ABOUT THEM.

Real-life versions of the Death Star are something for which we should be watchful. We know the ones we have seen in the past, and the ones we now see from far off. The Nazi machine, many elements of the Roman Empire, modern-day Somalia, the Rwandan genocide, and the Arab nations' continual hate of Israel. The hallmarks are anger, fear, and aggression (Does this sound familiar?) These emotions are often evoked by overwhelming majorities who collectively express anger and hate against a minority.

So what are we supposed to do? To begin with, sitting on a couch watching TV or playing a video game and never becoming aware of our world is a sin. An evil empire is stopped, changed, and transformed by simple people. Do we all have to be activists? It depends on your definition. In our minds, yes, we need to be active in pursuing what we think is right in government, religion, the arts—all aspects of society. The first task in accomplishing this goal is to "take the plank out of our own eye" (Matthew 7:3). This means acknowledging our own faults, our own sins, and asking for forgiveness from God as well as the person we have sinned against. Our own sins are involved in an evil empire in some way, either by the things we do or by those things that we neglect to do.

The second task is to always be mindful of our surroundings, a theme that primarily comes out in *Episode I: The Phantom Menace* and *Episode II: Attack of the Clones* when Obi-Wan Kenobi is teaching a young Anakin Skywalker. In democratic countries, we need to be particularly mindful during political elections. This is when evil people are most likely to deceive you into thinking that they are good. For example, if a candidate states that God wants him or her to be president or prime minister, etc., we need to be mindful that this is a tactic to get people to vote for that person. Such a statement is improvable and irresponsible. It does not even fit the character of God that we know from the Bible: "Since no man knows the future, who can tell him what is to come?" (Ecclesiastes 8:7). This verse rather goes against any such proclamation by a candidate. And, "Let us love not with words or tongue, but with actions and in truth" (1 John 3:18). This verse points to leading by showing, not by telling. To say it is God's will that he or she be president means that God directly revealed this to him or her, which is not biblical. Direct revelation comes to us as the Word of God, the Bible. A candidate could say that he or she thinks God is leading them to run for the office of president, but this then is a very different statement. We all do this. If we believe in God, then we act according to how we think he is leading us. Unfortunately, even if a candidate, or an incumbent, is just saying something as harmless as "I think God is leading me . . ." the result is the same as if he or she were maliciously lying to us; he or she is still saying it merely to get votes. If the candidate were completely dedicated to this idea, he or she would never mention this in public. Add to this argument that God did not even want his chosen people, Israel, to have a king besides himself and we start to get a picture that does not fit any notion that the candidate or incumbent is attempting to put over on us. Our being mindful of these things can lead us to one conclusion: that the candidate is being irresponsible. We owe it to ourselves and to freedom to speak out against this kind of misuse. Why was it that the founding fathers separated church and state in the first place? It is because religious authority has a long and glorious tradition of being unchecked, and as such, leads to corruption. The point is that being mindful of these things and challenging them helps to prevent Death Stars, evil empires, and rulers like Palpatine. Just recognizing these things, however, only amounts to a beginning. Not doing anything about evil can be as dangerous as condoning it. If the Bible is any indication, God sometimes judges whole cities and nations for not standing up against Death Stars and their makers.

The third task is to do something. The way we stand up to evil is also important. Doing something that seems good for the wrong motive can also be a sin. An obvious example is stopping unborn children from being killed. This is a good thing! However, killing adults, as in the bombing of an abortion clinic in the pursuit of saving unborn children, is wrong. Much more difficult is the present example of an election. What do you do with a candidate or a president who has either boldly lied to his country in order to get the votes to stay in power or is so deceived about self and God that he has declared a self-righteous infallibility? Or perhaps he has just done a very irresponsible thing, setting a terrible precedent, and needs to be held accountable for the sake of the country?

Take a different example. What do we do about corporations that, either through clandestine business practices or by limiting the flow of information, attempt to control us as well as the citizens of other countries? What do we do about governments that allow genocide on a part of their own population? There are two definite answers to these questions, though they are only a beginning and not the full answers. The first is to fast and pray, and the second is to not do nothing.

[7] In Ben's hovel, Luke hears about the Force for the first time. *Ch'i*, Christianity, and myth.

Ben — ". . . Vader was seduced by the dark side of the Force."

Luke — "The Force?"

Ben — "Well, the Force is what gives the Jedi his power. It's an energy field created by all living things. It surrounds us and penetrates us. It binds the galaxy together."

Episode IV: A New Hope

Is this real? The words seem to be a good description of the *ch'i* or *ki* in Zen philosophy. The idea is very beautiful; living things must have energy and must emanate it. We must be able to tap into it to some extent. There is more, though. This power that surrounds us and penetrates us has something to do with God, who is the Creator and sustainer of all life. It is the only way the Force can be as personally special as so many of us want it to be. However, there is no concept of a deity in this description, so how are they in any way similar? What they have in common is myth.

Mythology is concerned with archetypal spiritual truths represented in and by their fictional stories. If your religion is a myth only, then you are really set up. This is to say that if your religion finds its truth in mythology, and the truth of mythology is found in fictional universal truths, and these universal truths find their truth in your religion, then your world view can be very comfy because it answers itself. Of course, it is also a bit like a dog chasing its own tail. Those who believe in the one true God who actually exists, and who did, in reality, create the world, and who sent his Son who actually died for us have another sort of problem. Since we claim the myth of our belief to be real, we can get stuck in the reality of God's realness. In always defending the realness of our faith, it is possible for us to neglect defending the myth of our faith. The fact that followers of

Jesus are rooted in the actuality of God coming to earth, dying for our sins, and rising again is essential, even orthodox. Unfortunately, dwelling only on the realness can make for some seriously mirthless people, and this does not at all represent the joy or realness of myth. The core issue is that Christians tend to be afraid that metaphors outside of Christendom will spoil us, or lead us into apostasy. This is possible. However, not engaging in myth stories is to deny the universal truths that we all have in common.

So where exactly is the common ground between this Zen-sounding concept of the Force and a true God? A mystical energy that surrounds us, penetrates us, and binds the galaxy together is very interesting to me and it causes me to wonder if there is any reality to this. If God exists, then he undoubtedly created the world, and so this mystical energy resonates with the creation story in Genesis. In her book, *The Mind of the Maker*, Dorothy Sayers explains that in Genesis, when we read that God created us in his image, the only thing we know about God's image thus far in Genesis is that he creates.[5] So we are to understand that the image of God in us is that we are able to create. Although we cannot create out of nothing, as God does, Sayers explains that in every work of creation there is an earthly trinity that parallels the heavenly one. This metaphoric trinity is made up of Idea, Energy, and Power. Now this sounds very similar to Zen and the Force. Sayers shows us that the creative metaphor goes like this: Idea is Father, Energy is Son, and Power is Holy Spirit. If you were writing a book, she says, the Idea is the idea of your book. The Energy is the activity of writing and publishing the book—the process of making the book a material object. Power is the book as it is read and responded to, which is the communication of the Idea through the Energy (the physical book) to others as well as the writer. In *Star Wars* terms, then, the Force is not a literal metaphor for God, but for his image in the Jedi and in the *Star Wars* universe. The Idea of the Force is its mystical, unseen existence. The Energy is the use of it by the Jedi and the Sith—how the Force is used, and the way in which it is used. The Power of the Force is the effect its use and ideas have on individuals, groups, and the entire universe upon which it is used. The Force exists as an Idea (energy—little "e"—that exists in and around all living things) whether or not it is harnessed, practiced, or has any influence on the universe. Yet, a Jedi only comes to know about the Force (Idea) through the teachings of another Jedi (Energy), and thus learns to experience the Force (Power) for himself. A Jedi understands that all three are the Force, they exist together and there cannot be one without the other. They are the same, yet each one is distinct.

But there had to be a Jedi to begin with, otherwise we are again chasing our tails in circular logic. Could there have been, deep in the history of *Star Wars*, a Jesus archetype that originally brought knowledge of the Force to the Jedi?

> In the beginning was the Word, and the Word was with God, and the Word was God. He was with God in the beginning.
>
> (John 1:1)

A good way to relate to the real trinity of the Force is in St. Patrick's Breastplate prayer.

St. Patrick's Breastplate prayer

I bind unto myself today
The strong Name of the Trinity,
By invocation of the same
The Three in One and One in Three.

I bind this today to me
Forever by the power of faith,
Christ's incarnation;
His baptism in Jordan river,
His death on Cross for my salvation;
His bursting from the spiced tomb,
His riding up the heavenly way,
His coming at the day of doom,
I bind unto myself today.

I bind unto myself the power
Of the great love of cherubim;
The sweet "Well done" in judgment hour,
The service of the seraphim,
Confessors' faith, Apostles' word,
The Patriarchs' prayers, the prophets' scrolls.
All good deeds done unto the Lord
And purity of virgin souls.

I bind unto myself today
The virtues of the starlit heaven,
The glorious sun's life-giving ray,
The whiteness of the moon at even,
The flashing of the lightning free,
The whirling wind's tempestuous shocks,
The stable earth, the deep salt sea
Around the old eternal rocks.

I bind unto myself today
The power of God to hold and lead,
His eye to watch, His might to stay,
His ear to hearken to my need.
The wisdom of my God to teach,
His hand to guide, His shield to ward;
The word of God to give me speech,
His heavenly host to be my guard.

Against the demon snares of sin,
The vice that gives temptation force,
The natural lusts that war within,
The hostile men that mar my course;
Or few or many, far or nigh,
In every place and in all hours,
Against their fierce hostility
I bind to me these holy powers.

Against all Satan's spells and wiles,
Against false words of heresy,
Against the knowledge that defiles,
Against the heart's idolatry,
Against the wizard's evil craft,
Against the death wound and the burning,
The choking wave, the poisoned shaft,
Protect me, Christ, till Thy returning.

Christ be with me, Christ within me,
Christ behind me, Christ before me,
Christ beside me, Christ to win me,
Christ to comfort and restore me.
Christ beneath me, Christ above me,
Christ in quiet, Christ in danger,
Christ in hearts of all that love me,
Christ in mouth of friend and stranger.

I bind unto myself the Name,
The strong Name of the Trinity,
By invocation of the same,
The Three in One and One in Three.
By Whom all nature hath creation,
Eternal Father, Spirit, Word:
Praise to the Lord of my salvation,
Salvation is of Christ the Lord.

(Translated from the Gaelic
by Cecil Frances Humphreys Alexander, 1889.)

The Force—not the dark side, which I'll get to later—is so much like the above beckoning of Christ's presence in us. It is not just a neutral energy field that envelops everything like cosmic gravity or the glue of the universe. It is that, but there is more, much more. The Force is more than an impersonal power source. The Force is like God's Trinitarian creative image in us. And we witness the trinity of God's creative power in the world. The Idea of his creation is all around us, it emanates Energy from all living things because God made them, which therefore shout his glory (Power) as part of their innate nature. Leaves and plants shimmer and shake with God's glory. We all exude energy, radio frequencies, heat, light. The nature poets teach us about the romance of nature. God is in this romance, wooing us, wowing us, enticing us to get into right alignment with him, dominating nature in a right way by using and serving it. He wants us to use the Force of his image in us and in his creation for his glory.

[8] BAD GUYS ARGUING IN THE DEATH STAR CONFERENCE ROOM. THE GOOD-VERSUS-EVIL THING IS GOOD TO CELEBRATE WHEN REPRESENTED WELL.

Scene: In a conference room inside the Death Star, Admiral Motti and General Taggi are arguing over the threat posed by the Rebel forces to the Death Star and the entire Imperial Starfleet.

Episode IV: A New Hope

One of the characteristics of the Empire—this is a mythic story of good and evil after all—is the culture of power politics. Fear is the hallmark for this power politics and the manner in which one must jockey for power with his or her peers. Everyone is fighting for position, minding each other's business, and we know these people are bad even in the glossy, aristocratic setting of a Death Star conference room amid cool uniforms. Showing us the difference between good and evil is something that Lucas definitely means to convey. There are many articles, blogs, and books in which Christian opinion about *Star Wars* is the subject. Strangely, the good-versus-evil theme is one that these groups rarely acknowledge. Why is that? Can't Christians be *for* something once in awhile? Is it a bad thing to show affection for certain parts of pop culture? This is the most influential movie saga ever made for millions of people worldwide, and it is a tale of good versus evil. We read these fairy tales to our kids at night, as they were read to us, so why not embrace *Star Wars*? On a personal note, my wife and I have allowed our four-year-old son to see bits of *Star Wars* since he was born. Although he cannot really understand a lot of the plot and dialogue, the one thing he does understand at this highly impressionable age is the theme of good guys versus bad guys. Plus, our son's play imagination is really activated by *Star Wars*. Lucas put kid-tested characters such as R2-D2, C-3PO, the Ewoks, and Jar Jar Binks in *Star Wars* on purpose; they are like candy. If a child has characters that he or she likes, that are on the child's level, he or she will keep watching, and the child will learn to define good and bad, and he or she will want to be good, even if the child plays with the bad guy action figures and sometimes acts like that particular bad guy.

During this scene, we learn that the Republican Senate has just been permanently dissolved. We also learn that Darth Vader has the power to choke someone without physically touching him. Motti spouts off, saying, ". . . Your sad devotion to that ancient religion has not helped you conjure up the stolen data tapes, or given you clairvoyance enough to find the Rebel's hidden fort . . ." and Vader starts choking him, proving that Vader's sad devotion is at least strong enough to kill his opponents rather easily. It is also good to know what can and cannot be done in the *Star Wars* world, and with the Force; and Motti makes a good point. Vader is unable to find either the stolen data or the Rebel's base. These limitations are reminiscent of the verse used once already in reference to being wary of politicians claiming to be God's choice. Ecclesiastes 8:7, "Since no man knows the future, who can tell him what is to come?"

Vader choking Motti is symbolic of people who do not tolerate disagreement. In the other movies, there are many more examples of Vader's wrath when he does not like a decision someone has made, or if they disagree with him. I have had experiences with people very close to me that express anger in a way that reminds me of Darth Vader. They did not even want to tolerate the notion of disagreement because it messed up their plan for what should happen. If you had a point you were trying to make, they seemed to fear the outcome of the conversation, as if the changing of a plan because of your good idea or input might physically hurt them. Have you ever experienced that?

To see real-world frustrations in the fiction of *Star Wars* helps us understand what a person, even ourselves, is experiencing. Then we know how to pray for the person, or ourselves, because we know what is getting in our way. In the previous example, it is fear. There are, of course, other ways to discern this fear—psychology, spiritual discernment, intuition, books, learning from other movies, to name just a few. It is good to learn about as many of these disciplines as possible, although it is likely that who you are will resonate with one method more than another. Seeing truth in stories is a common trait for most everyone. Looking at *Star Wars*, or anything, in such an in-depth manner helps us to slow down and be thorough about our enjoyment of these films.

[9] Striking a balance instead of extremes, even when Stormtroopers slaughter and burn your aunt and uncle? You must be crazy.

When Luke discovers in *Episode IV: A New Hope* that stormtroopers murdered his aunt and uncle, he is angry, and rightly so. The difficulty with evil is that it often makes you want to do something evil in return. Revenge seems so right. This is why the apostle Paul said,

> "Do not take revenge, my friends, but leave room for God's wrath, for it is written: 'It is mine to avenge; I will repay,' says the Lord. On the contrary: 'If your enemy is hungry, feed him; if he is thirsty, give him something to drink. In doing this, you will heap burning coals on his head.' Do not be overcome by evil, but overcome evil with good."
>
> (Romans 12:19–21)

This is hard to take no matter how many times you hear it. Having faith that God will be just, and most likely not in the time frame you would like him to be, is very difficult. When Luke returns from seeing his aunt and uncle's place destroyed and their bodies burnt, he must have wanted to join Obi-Wan out of a desire for revenge. This desire for revenge is a conflict even through the final movie in the series. The murder of people whom Luke loves tempts him to want to murder others. This desire for revenge accomplishes what the dark side, what evil, wants. This is true in our world as well. We do not bring good into the world by repaying evil with evil (Romans 12:17). Again, there is a hard balance between knowing when to fight a dictator or a terrorist with arms and when to fight with love.

Luke is angry, sad, and distraught that the life he knows is changing so abruptly and violently. He clings to the back-handed blessing of the moving of the Force; if he had not removed the restraining bolt from R2-D2, and R2-D2 had not gone off on his own to find Obi-Wan, Luke would have died alongside Uncle Owen and Aunt

Beru. As Obi-Wan points out, the droids would most likely have fallen into the hands of the Empire. It would be easy for Luke to take the path of thinking that taking vengeance for vengeance's sake is the right way to go. However, he would have done it for the wrong motivations: anger, fear, aggression; the same things Yoda warns against in the next film of the series. Doing the right thing for the wrong reasons is still wrong. This is one reason why terrorism is wrong. If Luke acts out of his anger, he will move to the dark side of the Force as well. Having a right heart, a desire for truth, for good, is essential to purify one's motives in battle.

Now, had Obi-Wan taught Luke that he must forgive his enemies, Luke's task would be even more impossible, and perhaps even more true. Forgiveness, however, is something only the Force could help Luke accomplish.

[10] Luke and Ben at Mos Eisley. The Jedi concept of Place.

Old Ben and Luke, in their needy situation, meet up with Han Solo and Chewbacca, who also find themselves in a needy situation. Is this just another coincidence? Perhaps it is simply another convenient plot development device—or maybe the Force is involved in bringing them all together. In the fourth entry of this book, the Jedi concept of time is discussed, which is to say the idea of *when* in the classic five Ws of "who, what, where, when, why, (and how)." The Jedi concept of place is the idea of *where*. This ties in very closely to the idea of time. If either party had arrived at the Cantina a day or two earlier or later, they would have missed each other. Instead, Ben and Luke are in the right place at the right time to meet Han and Chewy. The fullness of place or *where*, to sound rather metaphysical about it, comes about in the fullness of time or *when* for them to find each other.

The deeper truth is that Luke will soon need the bravery and trueness of spirit shown by Han and Chewy when they arrive at the Death Star. And Han Solo certainly is hanging out with the wrong crowd—becoming involved in the Rebellion and the giving of self instead of selfishness—so his involvement with Luke is a backhanded blessing to Han.

Ben has faith that the right kind of people will present themselves in what, at first glance, appears to be a highly unlikely place—the seedy pilot's bar. There are many examples of the Jedi having a different concept of *place* than we might normally think is logical. Ben being on Tatooine all this time is a discipline of *place*. Tatooine was the place the Force wanted him to be (if the Force were personal). Obi-Wan would likely much rather have been fighting the Emperor and Darth Vader. The remainder of *Episode IV: A New Hope* is a veritable study in the coordination of Jedi time and place: Alderaan is blown up, but Luke rescues Princess Leia, who at that point is the only person who can lead them to the rebel base; the weakness of the Death Star is discovered in just enough time for Luke and the others to get to the approaching Death Star just seconds before it is able to destroy the Rebel base. However, the Jedi concept of place goes even further than that.

To jump ahead in the chronology of the films for a second, what Luke experiences on Dagobah in *Episode V: The Empire Strikes Back* is also a different perspective on *where*. Where Luke physically is in the universe does not matter; the fact that he is using the Force and growing in it causes him to have a presence in the Force and to a small extent feel what is going on with his friends. Luke's teachers understand this. Luke is young in the Force, and cannot understand the much deeper significance of Han, Chewy, and Leia's suffering. This is a trap that Vader has set for Luke, using the Force. Vader knows that wherever Luke is in the universe, Luke will sense that his friends are in trouble, but Luke will be unable to sense the extremely tenuous situations in which he finds himself. Essentially, Luke is the last Jedi, facing the much more powerful Vader long before Luke has the skills necessary to fight him. In short, Luke is ripe for the taking. Vader needs Luke physically in front of him in order to kill or coerce him, that much he cannot do in the spirit world of the Force. This is the reason why Vader tortures Han and Chewbacca without ever asking them any questions. Vader knows their pain will act like radio signals to Luke, whose young antennae of sensing things in the Force would pick them up and come after them.

One final note on this idea of place being everywhere and nowhere all at once for the Jedi. In *Episode I: The Phantom Menace*, when Qui-Gon and Obi-Wan are able to do the quick run thing to get away from the destroyer droids, this ability might also be a result of being so slow and so present in the now that a Jedi can develop the power to warp space and time so that being in front of the destroyer droids or being way down the hall from them is almost the same, and appears to our eyes as moving quickly.

[11] JEDI MIND TRICKS.
THE FORCE HAS A STRONG INFLUENCE
ON THE WEAK MINDED.

Obi-Wan uses the Jedi mind trick on imperial stormtroopers upon their arrival in Mos Eisley. He explains the Jedi mind trick to Luke, "The Force has a strong influence on the weak-minded."

In real life, it is rare when we can pass off the same thing that Obi-Wan did in the speeder. However, in different ways this type of activity happens all the time.

When we are convinced of a certain thing, it is usually easy to convince someone who is not so certain. Often, we also make use of the same tactics of subtle suggestion that Ben utilizes. Everywhere we see people with purpose getting to where they want to go, talking people into doing what the stronger-willed person thinks is best, etc. It is a true statement that your force of character has a strong influence on those with a weaker force of character. This is our will. Willing something to happen causes us to move in that direction. This is a powerful character trait often seen in many men and women who are getting things done, succeeding, and winning. The problem, at least in America, is that so many of these people break laws, eschew morality, and are ruthless to their neighbor so that they can win. This is a sign of the decline of our civilization. This happens when we love ourselves more than we love others. At this point, our influence on the weak-minded works for evil. Ironically, from a spiritual point of view this is when an evil force or spirit is actually having a strong influence on you, the weak-minded/weak-spirited. It is through selflessness that our spirit becomes strong, and can have a right influence on others. Influence is not control. We want to ". . . spur one another on toward love and good deeds" (Hebrews 10:24).

As humans, we can also be prey to real Jedi mind tricks. We would like to think that most of us are not weak-minded, but how many of us go for those $19.95 scams on TV? "But wait, there's more," they always say. Or the get-rich-quick schemes? How many of us go in for religious superstition without checking it out first? How about the TV evangelists? Isn't it enough that just looking at a show is a tip off to where they are putting their money: nice clothes, extravagant sets, make-up, jewelry. How dumb are we as a species? Abortion does not kill babies and does not injure women or men? What planet are we living on? One of my favorites, "You can become a god!" is what a few religions espouse. Yet, even the briefest scan of history (or even your own life) shows glaring sin and imperfection, which interjects realistic notions about how long it might take to reach self-deification. Then, just try to do something supernatural.

In *Huckleberry Finn*, who was Mark Twain talking about when he showed the townspeople originally believing the King's and the Duke's shenanigans, giving them money and lauding them? All of us, of course. Not one of us is immune to the silliness of being weak-minded sometimes.

> "Who is wise and understanding among you? Let him show it by his good life, by deeds done in the humility that comes from wisdom."
>
> (James 3:13)

Beware of the glossy and the glamorous.

[12] YIELD TO ADULTS AT PLAY.

It is a wonderful part of human nature to love hearing about and creating our own worlds. Imagination is so much a part of who we are that children instinctively use it when they play. No one has to teach them. The sheer fact that the *Star Wars* universe exists represents a rejoicing in the good of creation, in the goodness of play. God found his world good, and certainly George Lucas, the cast, and the crew found the world they created to be good as well. God wants us to be like him, which is very much a command to create, which involves play. God built us for this.

Unfortunately, school, the pressures of growing up, and the hard issues that adults have to face, like paying bills, really threatens our re-learning to play. Adults build up lists of *shoulds*. *Shoulds* are those things that we feel or are told to do out of a sense of obligation. Some of them are valid responsibilities. Others we allow to keep us from the tasks that we enjoy doing or might be called to do. You *should* take a responsible job, you *should* go to college, you *should* go to church, etc. It is possible that you are doing a thing because your *should* negates the reason to do it. This was very much the message of Jesus. Obeying the Jewish laws for the *should* of it denied the purpose of obeying them. For this reason, Jesus set us straight. Obeying the spirit of God's law honors God. If you do something willingly, you learn the purpose of it. If you do it out of coercion, because you *should*, you do not learn the reason or the wisdom behind it. The creation of *Star Wars* itself, as well as the actual worlds and creatures within the film series, is an example of letting go the control of our lives according to *shoulds*. Even George Lucas, when making the first *Star Wars* film, encountered much opposition and many *shoulds*. However, the *Star Wars* series is child's play, and it is adult's play. It stands as an encouragement to play.

Adult play is harder and more complicated than the play of a child, and more is required of our imaginations. An adult has to seek to play in the real world as well as the fantasy world, and this is not at all easy to do. When it is done properly, however, the imagination becomes the fuel for free societies.

[13] THE DEATH STAR: THE ACT AND IMAGE OF A COMPLETE LACK OF FAITH.
SENSING A GREAT DISTURBANCE IN THE FORCE.

Scene: In the Death Star, Princess Leia Organa resists the mind probe and makes an appearance in front of Grand Moff Tarkin so that he can extort the location of a secret Rebel base or blow up her peaceful home planet of Alderaan.

Leia   –   "The more you tighten your grip, Tarkin, the more star systems will slip through your fingers."

Episode IV: A New Hope

The act of creating a Death Star to control a population shows a lack of faith in society. Any government that seeks the simplicity of controlling people to any extreme—and the Death Star was more than a tad extreme—does this because its leaders think it is easier and better than working through the muddy situation of freedom. Ironically, these control measures do not end up creating the civilization that those same leaders wanted in the first place. China is a good example of this. Anakin struggled with having faith in society in Episodes II and III, as the Republic faced many problems. He ultimately failed to have faith in society, in the light side of the Force, and in freedom, causing the death of millions and the eclipse of a civilization during his reign with the Emperor—all with the first intent of saving it, and helping it.

The Death Star itself, the size of a small moon, steely gray and ominous, is a metaphor for the supreme weapon of a civilization. A society that seeks to control the population must strike fear in its citizens so it must have an image that people fear. The purpose of the Death Star was not to use it frequently, but to demonstrate its ability and then have it for everyone to see or hear about. Like the police in communist countries, you fear that any random act might bring them to your door and so you become less and less of who you are meant to be. This is the effect of a government that does not have faith.

Leia is pretty bold to state that star systems will slip through the fingers of the Empire. However, it tends to takes a long, long time for the power structure of an Empire to self-destruct. At the very least, the history of our own planet rather confirms the longevity of empires.

When the Death Star blows away Alderaan—a planet with no weapons or armies or defenses—there is not just the reality that this weapon can destroy whole planets, but it also takes the Empire's indiscriminate killing to a mass scale. The movie progresses quickly from there. However, the fact that a government just randomly obliterated millions of its own citizens in cold blood, if dwelled upon any longer than it was in the movie, would make us think that Leia's response was not extreme enough. Her whole body would have gone into shock for the sheer soulless terror of the destructive act.

[14] LIGHTSABER TRAINING ON THE MILLENNIUM FALCON. "REMEMBER, A JEDI CAN FEEL THE FORCE FLOWING THROUGH HIM."

Luke's only family has just been murdered. He is leaving his home planet, possibly forever, and this is perhaps his first venture into deep space. Obi-Wan is teaching him some weird tricks about becoming an ancient type of warrior called a Jedi. It is a wonder Luke is able to concentrate at all. As viewers, this is our first lesson on the Force, too. Until now, we have heard only slight mention of the Force and the Jedi philosophy. At this point in the film, in a brief pause between action sequences, we learn a little more.

Obi-Wan   –   "Remember, a Jedi can feel the Force flowing through him."
Luke   –   "You mean it controls your actions?"
Obi-Wan   –   "Partially, but it also obeys your commands."

Episode IV: A New Hope

This is like God directing us. Exactly how he directs us is partly logical, and partly a mystery. We have God's direct revelation to us in the Bible, his Word. When you are caught up in worship, though, it really feels like a force flowing through you. This is feeling the Holy Spirit's presence in a powerful way. We often hear of or see or experience an extreme version of this that perhaps has nothing to do with the Holy Spirit, and it causes many of us to want to stay away from anything charismatic or Holy Spirit-y. The Bible also says we have to test the spirits (I John 4:1) so that we don't turn what is originally beautiful into something profane. Striking a balance in charismatic worship can be a difficult thing to do because it is an exercise of the warm heart, which can make it hard for the cold mind to test the spirits. In *God in the Dock*, C.S. Lewis makes this distinction.

"While we are loving the man, bearing the pain, enjoying the pleasure, we are not intellectually apprehending Pleasure, Pain, or Personality. When we begin to do so, on the other hand, the concrete realities sink to the level of mere instances of examples: we are no longer dealing with them, but with that which they exemplify. This is our dilemma: either to taste and not know or to know and not to taste; or, more strictly, to lack one kind of knowledge because we are in an experience or to lack another kind because we are outside it. As thinkers, we are cut off from what we think about; as tasting, touching, willing, loving, hating, we do not clearly understand. The more lucidly we think, the more we are cut off: the more deeply we enter into reality, the less we can think. You cannot study Pleasure in the moment of the nuptial embrace, nor repentance while repenting . . ."[6]

(*God in the Dock,* "*Myth Became Fact,*" C.S. Lewis)

Charismatic worship is like the experience of pleasure, or feeling the Force flow through you. If mystic powers and supernatural stuff is what you are interested in, this is a good place to find it. The problem is that if you do not know Christ as your savior, you can't get the real thing. This is no private club, it is in fact the exact opposite—all powers available to you are in plain sight, and even the most simple-minded person can use them. To use a drug reference, it is the difference between getting a slight buzz and injecting it up your veins. No matter who we are, we have at least a little curiosity about things outside of our natural world, things supernatural from the spirit world. Worship of the true God, as well as other spiritual disciplines that will be explored later, are total spiritual trips and give us a taste of the reality we long for in the metaphor of the Force.

This is a concern for those cool minds in the church. The Bible teaches us about Pentecost and a little about spiritual gifts like tongues and prophesy, but it is a sticky issue, and they would rather stay away from it altogether. Revolving around one aspect of God, as many denominations do, gives the world the advantage of really learning about him in ways we discover and learn through these specific strengths of denominations. However, it leaves many parishioners of that denomination feeling as if they need something more. If a church is big on theology and developing the mind of Christ, which is thinking in the ways that Jesus Christ thought, then it is likely not to be so big on the charismatic gifts. If a church is good at charismatic gifts, it is possible they are not so good at theology. This often creates a real imbalance in the church service. C.S. Lewis compares the difference between book knowledge and experience to a kiss. This goes for the present analogy as well. Some people only like to kiss, others like talking or reading about kissing, but most of us prefer doing both—which is a problem for many modern Christian churches.

Feeling the Force flowing through us is a good metaphor for the Holy Spirit's work in us as we worship. In this capacity, the church is very feminine, receiving encouragement as we practice giving glory to God. It is the practice of the church as the metaphorical bride of Christ.

Feeling the Force is also a good metaphor for creative work. The end product is often better than what we are able to do by ourselves. Creative work could be defined as anything from the realm of banking to fine art to dirt-bike racing; anything under the sun. Just like worship, however, creative work can also be ruined. Just as with the Force, a balance is needed. You can think you are listening to the muse and really ruin a story or a painting. Quite possibly, the better we listen to the muse, to the critics, and to ourselves the better a work we are able to make.

Luke asks if the Force controls you. In the same way, does the Holy Spirit control us in those moments of worship or creativity? No, we are still ourselves, and yet we are more than just ourselves. How do we know when we are going too far, or not far enough? Wisdom is a big help in knowing the difference.

Right after Obi-Wan teaches Luke this lesson, he feels the great disturbance in the Force as Alderaan blows up and he is almost physically thrown to the floor. Perhaps it is grace that we do not feel this in our own world. Some people have learned to be so connected to the Holy Spirit that they are given certain similar impressions and are guided to pray because of this. Like Obi-Wan though, we do not know the future or even the present other than where we exist.

We cannot tell the future or the present, and we are unwise to try to conjure or divine the future. The Bible cautions against witchcraft of every kind. The nugget of truth that real life witches and wizards seek, however, is often the world of the supernatural. Supernatural gifts do exist in this life, and these are given by the Holy Spirit. The ones that might seem more glamorous to us are actually the ones we are told about in 1 Corinthians 12, 13, and 14 are not as high rank-ing. Love is the purpose of these gifts, then Faith, and Hope. The gifts are ranked from most important to least: apostleship, prophesy, and discernment of the prophesy, teaching, miracle working, heal-ers, helpers, administrators, speakers, and interpreters of tongues. The purpose of powers in the Force also seems to be love, though the Jedi do not explicitly state this. Certainly their opposite—the Sith—are motivated by hate.

Obi-Wan feels the disturbance inside of him, and it seems almost like Extra-Sensory Perception or ESP. Is ESP in one of the above gifts? ESP is very closely related to intuition, and intuition is tradi-tionally thought of as a very feminine quality. Is this part of the gift of prophesy?

[15] Luke practices the lightsaber with his blast shield down.
Letting go of your conscious self in the Western world.

Zapped by the remote, Luke takes a break and has a conversation with Han Solo about his skepticism and gun-slinging philosophy; then Obi-Wan places a helmet with a blast shield on Luke's head.

Obi-Wan   –   "This time, let go of your conscious self and act on instinct."

Luke   –   "But with the blast shield down, how can I see?"

Obi-Wan   –   "Your eyes can deceive you, don't trust them. Stretch out with your feelings."

Luke does stretch out with his feelings, and he is able to parry with the remote without seeing anything with his eyes.

Luke   –   "You know, I could almost see the remote."

Obi-Wan   –   "That's good. You've taken your first step into a larger world."

Episode IV: A New Hope

This is a beautiful scene, even though in real life it is an incomplete idea. Letting go of our conscious self is so real, so directly applicable. In any endeavor of man, the ones who often accomplish what they are after are the ones who let go of their ego.

Look at a tennis player. If she lets her ego get in the way, her love of her celebrity, the love of how good she is, she becomes nothing. You must lose yourself to find yourself. To become something you must become nothing. To play tennis well you must let go of your overly conscious self and fully commit to your work.

Our eyes can deceive us, Obi-Wan warns, and this is true. Jesus even says that those who believe in him without seeing him are blessed by this faith. Here is why the picture of Luke with the blast shield down is not as complete an idea in our universe: because it is also true that our eyes can help us, and save us. Even in the sense that this text is meant, that of using the Force; with our eyes we can see things about who people are, and we observe how our universe behaves and how it is made up. In teaching about how our hearts are with whatever we treasure, Jesus instructs us not to store up earthly treasures or money. He says,

> The eye is the lamp of the body. If your eyes are good, your whole body will be full of light. But if your eyes are bad, your whole body will be full of darkness. If then the light within you is darkness, how great is that darkness!
>
> (Matthew 6: 22,23)

Our eyes can tell much about what we and others treasure, and that is valuable information to a Jedi's work. The Force would be a fuller concept if it had acknowledged this.

[16] THE FORCE OF HAN SOLO

Han Solo does not believe in "hokey religions and ancient weapons. There is no mystical energy field that controls my destiny." His world view is about luck, "simple tricks and nonesuch." This is the opposite from what the Jedi believe, though their adventures seem to bear out that there is a little truth in both philosophies. Luke and Han use the simple tricks of disguising themselves as stormtroopers transferring Chewbacca from prison cellblock 1138 in order to get to where Princess Leia is held. To counter these tricks and nonesuch, it could hardly have been coincidence or chance that gets them out of the bungle. The droids act as the (unknowing) agents of the Force in getting Han, Luke, Chewy, and Leia out of the garbage chute they end up in, and Obi-Wan's wise trusting of the Force helps him disable the tractor beam and provides his sacrificial distraction so the rest can all get onto the *Millennium Falcon* and fly away. Any good epic story of good versus evil probably uses a little of both philosophies. Symbolic of Han's influence, along with his lightsaber, Luke also carries "a good blaster at his side," as Han Solo recommends.

Isn't Han's lone pragmatism actually its own kind of hokey religion? He seems to realize this in later movies, and he takes steps into a larger world as he matures.

The Force of Han Solo is more than just "simple tricks and nonesuch," however. Han is a true soul in his quick loyalty to the Rebel cause. Although he tells Leia that he is "just in it for the money, sister," he charges down hallways alone while screaming, helps Leia and Luke in the garbage compactor, rushes in at the last second to help Luke fly down the trench (after Han has already received his reward), and keeps an extremely honorable and trustworthy companion, Chewbacca. If he were only the sum of what he said he believed in, then he would not have been as big a character as we know him.

[17] THE TANGIBLE QUALITY OF USING THE FORCE.

Have you ever said something that another person does not like? One time I felt a cold, angry spirit come over the phone when I confronted a friend of mine with something he was not doing. I tangibly felt a cold grip on me that I believe was the mal-intent of his anger upon me. Was this real, or was it my interpreted meaning of what he was saying? In that moment it felt real, and not a fabrication of my imagination. If he were using the light side of the Force, as in if he were exercising love in disagreeing with me, it would have felt warm, like he was listening and considering my words, then thoughtfully disagreeing. Instead I felt that he had only called so that I would commiserate with him and validate his inaction. When I expressed my own opinion, which was not even extremely different from his, I felt immediate rage come at me. He was at this moment very strong in the Force in that I literally felt his anger. The issue with the dark side is that as you seek to control others it controls you, always, and bad things are always the result. Although the show of the dark side appears strong, it is really a weakness; my friend allowed himself to be controlled. It would be wise of us to remember that the dark side is an idea from *Star Wars*; the dark power in our world is the devil and his demons, and inside of us in that we use God's image for evil.

In *Episode IV: A New Hope*, this was never more clearly seen as it was in Darth Vader. For some reason he was not quick to kill Leia on the Death Star—did he feel the Force was strong in her? Even admirals cowered in the presence of Darth Vader. They could feel the atmosphere he brought with him, like the atmosphere my friend allowed to be created. Leia is so strong-willed that she pushes his presence back. She defies him, even when she knows he can kill her just by thinking it.

Darth Vader also feels the presence of Obi-Wan when the Death Star reels in the *Millennium Falcon*. We create a spiritual and emotional climate wherever we go. Have you ever fallen in love? There is an energy field between two lovers that can be seen, even though it is invisible. The attraction is very hard to hide.

In a busy city, you can feel the focus of all the people you pass on the street. The focus of these people is not often on the street. Instead, each person is usually focusing thoughts deep within him- or herself. The energy created by the bustle of everyone is present, and that quality is very much a part of the personality of a city. Much of a person's life in the city is spent around random people; in transit you are with those whom you don't mean to be with, in a place where you are only passing through. Portable electronic entertainment devices take people even farther away from a physical present tense. Then there is the traffic, inside the city and out. Many people sit alone in cars that are all stuck together in urban gridlock. Even so, there is a great energy and *Gemein* created by the seeming chaotic movement of a city.

Other examples: Have you ever felt the overwhelming love, acceptance, and embrace from a mother figure? Have you ever experienced the magic nature of a forest, or a desert, or the ocean, or a lake . . .? These are all proofs for the energy created by all living things, binding us together. These are also proofs of a Creator. It is OK that Lucas decided not to make this an explicitly Christian myth, with precise metaphors. In fact, it is probably better. Christendom might have ruined it with overuse. Still, a fuller representation of the one, true God would enhance the story. It almost seems there is so much in this series that gravitates around the idea of God, just without mentioning him.

[18] "Your destiny lies along a different path from mine."

"Your destiny lies along a different path from mine," Obi-Wan says to Luke. When the *Millennium Falcon* is tractor-beamed into the Death Star, Obi-Wan Kenobi senses Darth Vader's presence. He knows, too, that Vader can sense his presence. Knowing that Luke is Vader's son, Obi-Wan quickly surmises that to protect Luke he must go somewhere alone. He intuits that Vader will be attracted to his presence and that they must, therefore, meet and fight. It is with this knowledge that Obi-Wan understands that his destiny is separate from Luke's.

What is the right way to see destiny? God does predestine us all to know him. He also knows most of us won't choose him. We can control our destiny in that we can choose to do good things to help us become better people, and we can choose to do things that help us decline. Of course, what we do every day of our lives affects if we are rich or poor, smart or dumb, wise or foolish. It is also true, then, that if we get drunk every day, are constantly crass, selfishly obstinate, sexually immoral and refuse to educate ourselves, etc. we are not suddenly going to be healthy, wealthy, and wise. It's like everything we do and everything we are is like in a video game where you build up points or powers or skills . . . but you can build up good ones that help toward good goals or bad ones that help toward bad goals, and there is not a lot of crossover. Then, in the video game of our lives we can only go so far on our own. We are finite just like the character we play on our favorite game. We need help from the devil if we are going to be really evil. And we need help from God if we are going to be good. Odd thing about this game of ours is that the pursuit of good (righteousness, holiness, etc.) is that it kind of works opposite to the direction we might think is forward. It just does not make sense that if you want to be the greatest you must be the least, but it is true in the myth story of *Star Wars*, and this points to the true myth of God coming to us. Maybe this is working out our destiny, but the example of Obi-Wan in relation to destiny is curious, compelling and it strikes a true chord.

Obi-Wan felt the force leading him to a confrontation with Vader and it seems he understood before the fight that he must allow himself to be killed so that the light side of the force could become stronger—however that works. But there is an element to which Obi-Wan and the way he allowed himself to be killed, then became a spirit able to talk to Luke, was like Christ's death, his ascension, and sending of the Holy Spirit to us. In fact, in early versions of the screenplay, this was Lucas' intent (*Skywalking*, p. 145, cited in *Unlocking the Mystery of the Force* by Frank Allnutt).

Obi-Wan helps me imagine Philippians 1:20–21,

> "I eagerly expect and hope that I will in no way be ashamed, but will have sufficient courage so that now, as always, Christ will be exalted in my body, whether by life or by death. For to me, to live is Christ, and to die is gain."

Maybe this is the right way to see destiny. Self-sacrifice, whether resulting in life or in death, is what we are to aim for. In doing this, we shortcut any selfish desires that we seem to involve our lives with, hoping fate and destiny will smile on us and make us great people.

Towards this understanding, it is also good to mention that as much dying by Vader's lightsaber is a sacrifice, the way Obi-Wan watches over Luke from afar on that dusty, remote planet of Tatooine for twenty years is also a very great sacrifice. Some days sacrifice looks like a quick lightsaber through the belly; some days—most days probably—it is a lowly, dusty thing.

[19] "THE FORCE WILL BE WITH YOU . . . ALWAYS."

"The Force will be with you . . . always," Obi-Wan says to Luke right after he tells him that he is going to shut down the tractor beam alone and that Luke's destiny lies on a different path than his own.

This quote and, "May the Force be with you" are *Star Wars* blessings to each other. In my religious tradition the priest says, "The Lord be with you" to which the congregation responds, "and also with you." I cannot tell you how often I hear, "May the Force be with you" while watching the movies and instinctively I want to respond, "and also with you." Talk about your actual translation from the world of *Star Wars* to our real world. It is not just similar in text and meaning, it is similar in intent. This is an exercise of faith. We believe that our saying these words is an actual blessing upon people. If we are only flesh and blood, this is a silly thing to say. If we believe that we can ask God to bless people by being present with them and that he will do so by our asking—this is saying quite a lot about who humans are and what we can do.

If you have no idea what I am talking about, try saying, "The Lord be with you" aloud to someone. Even though the word *lord* carries an outdated meaning in the western world, saying those words is powerful. Compare this to when you swear, and then to when you swear using one of God's names. If you try this, you will feel the power and the meaning of the words; it is much more than just a socialized phenomenon of speech.

[20] "Escape is not his plan. The Force is with him."

"Escape is not his plan. The Force is with him," Darth Vader states to Admiral Motti on the Death Star when they realize that Obi-Wan is on board. When teams or individuals play each other in sports, can't you feel the sway, the swing, the momentum of the game is often with one side? We say, "It's going his or her or their way." This is not really saying that one team is in God's favor more than another, but that for some reason, more than just all the logical ones, there is something else, something unexplainable about putting one's will into something. We do create our own reality to a great extent, and in putting our will toward something our resolve is very powerful. This is another aspect of the Force being with you. If you are on a team, everyone has to feel that desire, to put that will in place of their own desires and drive together toward the goal.

[21] A COST/BENEFIT ANALYSIS OF BEN KENOBI'S SACRIFICE.

Ben's sacrifice: Greater love has no one than this, that he lay down his life for his friends (John 15:13). If we only saw the first *Star Wars* film up to the point of Ben's sacrifice, if we did not know his future, we would be rightly puzzled over why Ben was so willing to give up his life. This is like not knowing our own future. What is served by Ben's death? In that moment of decision, if we had had a business plan, or a cost-benefit analysis, or used a tactical and strategic decision matrix, it would never make sense to sacrifice a Jedi Master for a princess, droids with a blueprint of the Death Star, a boy straight off the farm, a smuggler, and a Wookiee. Obi-Wan was a better choice to battle the Empire over the others put together. But the Force, like God in our lives, has a plan that is greater than us, and sometimes it looks illogical from our angle. We can't see it or know it, but we do know that we are a part of it, and that our decisions influence it. That is how life is. There are times when his leading does not seem the most logical, certainly not the most business or economically savvy thing to do. Ben did not doubt his course of action; he trusted the Force.

Trusting and having faith is a combination of preparing, learning, growing, using every tool we have available—thinking, feeling, learning and using spiritual discipline, financial planning, saving, innovating, creating—everything under the sun, and after all that we may sense he is leading us to do something crazy or illogical. If Ben was thinking of himself he might have thought that willingly allowing himself to be killed by Darth Vader was ridiculous. Crazy and illogical is not to be confused with sensing we should do something that is against our nature. Crazy and illogical could be the deception of the dark side, and sometimes they seem very similar. For example: plenty of people in all denominations say "God told me this," or "He is leading me to do this." Plenty of people in other religious traditions say similar things. To know whether something you feel inside you is right or not, you check it with the Bible. Is it consistent with the character of God? Knowing about the character of God is not an immediate download. It takes time, practice, wisdom. The practice of the spiritual disciplines goes a long way in helping you become more Jedi about making decisions—especially major life decisions. Ben Kenobi's Jedi training prepared him for the decisions he made.

Creating art is a similar process of gaining as much technical experience and knowledge as you can, then letting yourself be taken by the spirit of the story, the painting, the music, etc. Afterwards you judge your own work, and allow others to as well. The better a judge of truth you are, the more equipped you are to improve your work and become a better artist. As you've read already, this takes developing your warm heart and your cold mind.

[22] "IF YOU STRIKE ME DOWN, I SHALL BECOME MORE POWERFUL THAN YOU CAN POSSIBLY IMAGINE." THE POWER PARADOX OF CHRIST, THIS IS.

The power paradox of Christ, this is:

> For me to live is Christ, and to die is gain.
>
> (Philippians 1:21)

> Whoever finds his life will lose it, and whoever loses his life for my sake will find it.
>
> (Matthew 10:39)

> I have been crucified with Christ and I no longer live, but Christ lives in me. The life I live in the body, I live by faith in the Son of God, who loved me and gave himself for me.
>
> (Galatians 2:20)

> My grace is sufficient for you, for my power is made perfect in weakness.
>
> (2 Corinthians 12:9)

These are all hard truths.

When we give up our lives symbolically, metaphorically, or physically, we do not know if there is more to the story. We must have faith that a decision to do something against the protection of self is strangely, ironically, the only way to protect one's self for eternity. However, there is more to the story, both in life and in death, as we see in Ben Kenobi.

The diversion to hold Vader at bay plays to Vader's pride. Vader allows the rag-tag band to get away with R2-D2 holding the blueprints to the Death Star. He and the other military leaders consciously take a risk that the Rebels will not find anything to exploit, or be able to do anything with that information if they do find a weakness. They plant a homing device on board the *Millennium Falcon* in hopes they will be led to the secret Rebel base. What Vader must not understand is Ben. Why does Ben stay aboard the Death Star? Why does

he allow Vader to strike him down? Does Ben simply decide to sacrifice himself for the team? Why does Ben warn Vader that he will
become more powerful than Vader can possibly imagine?

This distraction prevents Vader from feeling the Force flow, and in
this instance, also prevents Vader from discovering, no doubt to his
overwhelming surprise, that his son lives, is present, and in close
proximity. Ben's sacrifice in life also works out to be brilliant strategy.
Vader is thinking only in the dimension of logical cost/benefit analysis. He has Ben, his troops will track the ship, and soon the Death
Star will destroy the entire Rebel army. He must despise the Rebels
and Ben for being unworthy opponents who are so easy to destroy.
What he misses is his son, perhaps the only person besides Ben who
can use the Force in such a way as to exploit the tiny weakness of the
Death Star and destroy it. Vader's action sets the Empire back years,
kills thousands of bad guys, bolsters the Rebel Alliance, and brings
the Jedi back to the universe.

Vader's failure gets worse. Ben surrenders, salutes, and Vader slices
Ben through. Oddly enough, Ben's body disappears. We know from
subsequent *Star Wars* movies that this is not the manner in which
all Jedi die. When Ben tells Vader that he will become more powerful than Vader could possibly imagine, it is no false threat. Vader
sets Ben (Obi-Wan) Kenobi's spirit free to become a part of the living Force. Ben learned about life through death during his exile on
Tatooine.

Ben Kenobi vanishes when hit by Vader's lightsaber, and this is
also similar to our physical death. People who have faith in Jesus do
not physically vaporize like Kenobi, but spiritually we kind of do;
the process of having faith in Jesus as the Christ is the actual death of
our sinful spirit. This happens while our body is still living. In that
moment when Christ's Spirit comes into us, our old spirit dies and
we receive a new eternal spirit. When the time comes for our physical body to die, Christ's Spirit has already given us our new eternal
spirit, and the Spirit is with us, so physical death actually allows us
to be reunited with Christ more fully (2 Corinthians 5:8). In this
sense physical death is more like enhanced life than a taking away
of life; very similar to Kenobi's death in most respects.

[23] Luke zooms down the trench in the Death Star: A perfect metaphor for the practice of faith.

When Luke pilots his X-wing down the trench of the Death Star, the Death Star is within seconds of launching its planet-destroying blast. Most of the other fighters have already been annihilated and Luke's best friend is gunned down, leaving Luke as the only Rebel Alliance pilot remaining in the trench. Darth Vader and two of his special wing men are closing in right behind Luke, the last hope of the Rebels. What does Luke do at this critical moment? Does he become too distraught over the loss of his childhood friend Biggs to go on? No. Does he lose concentration with three very imposing TIE fighters bearing down on his X-wing, his death an imminent certainty? No. Instead, he responds to the sound of Ben Kenobi's voice inside his head.

Ben   —   Use the Force, Luke. (Pause) Let go, Luke! (Longer Pause) Luke, trust me.

Episode IV: A New Hope

With the future of the universe dramatically hanging on this one moment, Luke turns off his navigational computer and targeting device that would allow him to fire a small proton torpedo into the extremely small, unprotected vent opening that was the Death Star's only weakness. This action is ludicrous, if not for the Force. Han Solo and Chewbacca, aboard the *Millennium Falcon*, race in at the last moment, before Vader pushes a trigger to kill Luke, and fire a blast that sends Vader's spacecraft spinning wildly off into deep space. Luke then is able to focus his energy on targeting the exhaust port manually, his eyes and hands guided by the Force. He hits the impossible target at the very last moment possible, and streaks away to escape the devastating blast as the Death Star explodes.

This is the single best demonstration of how to practice faith that I have ever seen. Here's the interpretation: you are willing to do the work God draws you to do. Life's distractions come at you fast and furious. The devil will do anything to distract you. You use all the technology that man is able to muster, all the knowledge, all the skills, and all the abilities. You use all the assets that are available to you, and still it is not enough. No matter how much technology we ever have, no matter how much we ever train or learn, we come to moments when we understand that a task is impossible. What must be done we cannot accomplish on our own. We ask for help from a higher power whom we hope is out there to somehow come to our aid in this moment of crisis. Finally, we win, or reach the goal, or do the impossible. There is a great mystery in our doing great works, both large and small. What connects our "best we can do" ends with the beginning of success is God. The work takes faith. The practice of faith is the reason why the journey is as important as the destination.

For example, our knowing God is a work that, ironically, we cannot do on our own. Neither science nor theology will ever prove the existence of God. It is good for science to continue. It is good for theology to continue. In fighting the first Death Star, it is better for Luke to use an X-wing fighter than a bicycle. The more scientific knowledge we obtain, the more we know about the universe. The further we go in our study of God and what he says about himself, and the more we observe him at work in our world, the more we know about God. If God exists, then he certainly created the universe, and mankind along with it. He knows the universe and every person that has ever lived. If God exists, he must want us to know more, more, and more about everything. Like Luke in the trench, however, our abilities will always be limited. We must use the Force to "practice being sure of what we hope for and certain of what we do not see" (Hebrews 11:1).

Here is a more mundane example. You have TV, movies, games, a house, cars, music, religion, social groups, money, a job, sexual temptations, hobbies, personal hang-ups, injuries, careers, etc., that are all trying to distract you from loving your kids, your spouse, and yourself. All these distractions can also prevent you from knowing and loving God more deeply. How do you live?

We are all racing down that same trench on the surface of the Death Star with seconds to go before life blows the ones we love into astro dust. Darth Vader's hand is on the trigger, ready to blast us into nothingness. Our task is to launch a proton torpedo down a shaft that is six feet wide from a distance of a half mile even as we travel at hundreds of miles an hour in order to save our universe. There just ain't no way, no how.

But God did not just wind some clock. He did not predetermine our fate then leave. Instead, along comes God's personal and timely blessing. In Luke's case it came in the form of a renegade unbeliever, Han Solo, who directs a laser blast at Vader's TIE fighter that sends the villain flying. Then the Holy Spirit is like Ben Kenobi, who directs us to turn off the very last part of our technical world, the minutiae of a torpedo targeting system that symbolizes total faith in man. Then Ben says, "Use the Force, Luke."

In like fashion, God says to us today,

> Lean not on your own understanding, in all your ways acknowledge me, and I will make your paths straight.
>
> (Proverbs 3:5–6)

Han and Chewbacca fly in and blast Vader away. Han says, "You're all clear, kid. Now blow this thing and we can all go home." From out of nowhere, God's extra providence and help clear obstacles, allowing us to once again concentrate on the target even as life and all its details start flying around us. We practice God's presence just as Luke feels the Force in the X-wing before he targets the torpedo. He is—we are—supernaturally led. The one shot in a million happens! The super-evil monstrosity of the Death Star blows up just before it can destroy the Rebel base. The mighty Empire suffers a major defeat at the hands of a tiny, insignificant Rebel band.

What we learn is that it is good to take all the technology, all the skills, all the abilities that we have available to us, learn them, master them, then apply them to our task. We try as hard and as smart as we can to accomplish something, but it is never enough. There is always that impossible part of a work that cannot happen without God's help, whether we know it, know him, or even believe in him.

Understanding this metaphor can help us understand that we are flawed. We will never create some science that disproves or proves God. We are never going to create some technological device that eliminates all suffering. We are not evolving into some master race that no longer sins. God's help is always necessary, and our practice of faith—much like Luke using the Force in the Death Star's trench—is always required.

[24] HAN SOLO IS LIKE JESUS, ESPECIALLY WHEN IT COMES TO YOUR SUBCULTURE.

Han Solo is the archetypical renegade. Luke Skywalker and Ben Kenobi do not know if they can trust him. Han believes in himself, not the Force. He is unconventional by nature and is admittedly "in it for the money" in terms of the life's adventures.

It is easy for people who belong to subcultures—especially religious ones—to know and socialize only with those people who share the same beliefs. This is human nature, and it is not an altogether pejorative habit. However, this kind of exclusivity can create stagnation in a subculture. Even in the brief relationship that develops between Ben Kenobi and Luke Skywalker, there is a sudden subculture created when Ben teaches Luke about the Force; and together they immediately push against the uncivilized philosophies of the reckless Han.

When Ben leaves on his own mission within the Death Star, Han and Luke are forced to work together. Luke realizes it is his duty to get Princess Leia out of prison. Han believes it is his duty to stay alive, which means escaping from the Death Star. Luke taunts him with a monetary reward that Han might expect if he rescues the princess, and Han agrees, as much out of detesting the act of hiding as for a chance to earn more money. Han and Chewbacca go much further than mercenary work, however, and by the end of the movie, they save Luke from Darth Vader in a renegade, unforeseen, and unplanned fashion.

Luke experiences the validity of Han's bravery and immediate action even as Han learns the value of giving up of self, a virtue of the Force. In the same way, it is valuable for those in a subculture to eagerly seek out opportunities to meet, listen to, converse with, and become friends with people from other subcultures. This is particularly important in America, where it seems we are increasingly becoming more and more segmented into subcultures, outside of religion perhaps more than inside a shared belief system. The all-time king of dirt biking, for example, most likely is a virtual unknown to anyone outside of the dirt-biking world. Wouldn't that person's expertise be valuable in other disciplines, just as Han's experiences are valuable to Luke? America's different subcultures are becoming so well organized and developed that many of us are able to remain inside our circles quite comfortably without any outside influences.

It is part of God's love for the world—and his sense of humor—that he throws us together at times with so-called renegades from outside our safety zones. This practice can really help us, just as it helps the Rebels, as a whole, and Luke and Han, as individuals. Christians have Muslims around them, Muslims have Jews around them, Jews have Christians around them, and on and on. "But what they believe isn't true!" we are tempted to say. The sub-text in our minds can often be, "Samaritans can't be good."

Jesus is not only a savior archetype but also a renegade-type character. He does not belong to any one religious practice. The Christian church, of course, supposedly worships Jesus as God's Son, and Jesus does say, "No man comes to the Father except through me." But I have been in many, many Christian churches, and as boring and lifeless as some of them have been, I am led to the conclusion that although we all must face Jesus someday, this in no way implies that "No one gets to the Father except through a Christian church." The assumption is that Jesus belongs to Christians. A better theology is that people belong to Jesus if they choose to, and a church belongs to Jesus if its members live by his words. As we see so often evidenced in the headlines of today, as well as in our review of history, members, leaders, and the Christian religion as a whole does not at times act like Jesus at all. Jesus is the Christ, and anyone who believes this will likely have his or her religion challenged, even and especially those in the Christian tradition.

Because Jesus says we must go through him, it means that people of all religions must put up with a Han Solo-like character. This is uncomfortable to hear, and it tends to make us angry if we don't believe it is true. The character of Jesus, as we see him in the Bible, does not belong to one subculture. He demonstrates the true meaning of Jewish law—he was the one who wrote it after all—and to non-Jews, he is the one our ancestors were looking for in the unknown god statue, or the creator of the Tao, or the Caesar of Caesars.

Today he does not side with one Protestant denomination over another, and he does not check with the Pope before sending his Spirit to us. Jesus sticks out of the mythic tradition of religion as much as he defines it. The realness of Jesus is the fulfillment of the realness of myth. He wants people of all religions to believe in him, not just the so-called Christian faiths. That is the sticking-out part. Jesus will transform and renew any religion that allows him to do so.

We love subcultures. Is the Catholic Church acting like the Israelites of the Old Testament in its desire for a kingly figure such as the Pope? In the evangelical tradition, is a rich preacher a danger sign? Jesus acted a certain way while he was on earth, and that example is not one I often see emulated by church leaders. Christians often find it is easier to create an Empire of belief in Jesus than to personally obey him.

Han Solo ends up acknowledging the Force to a certain extent, but he also teaches the Rebels a thing or two, even as he instructs Luke the Jedi. Han Solo's immediate reaction to being caught in the tractor beam is "They're not getting me without a fight," even though Obi-Wan advises Han, "There are alternatives to fighting." Eventually Han and Chewy do realize their inevitable opportunity to fight, and their bravery is invaluable—and Luke notices this.

The Rebel Alliance also changes because of this new perspective. Like Han, Lando Calrissian has the same reckless abandon when it comes to fighting. In *Episode VI: Return of the Jedi*, Lando sees that the Rebel forces are trapped between the Imperial Fleet and Death Star II in such a way that Death Star II can pick them off one by one. Instead of retreat, which is what Admiral Ackbar advises, Lando wants to charge directly in among the Empire's fleet of Star Destroyers so that a blast from Death Star II would at least destroy the Empire's ships as well. Lando's opinion seems to be, "If today is the day we die, let's kill as many of the enemy as possible." This unflagging devotion to the cause allows Han time enough to destroy the shield generator and the full mission is accomplished.

[25] A small band of Rebels is strikingly similar to the early Christian church.

Finally, in *Episode IV: A New Hope,* there is an interesting parallel to Christianity in the comparison of the early Christian church to a small band of Rebels who seek to conquer an evil Empire that is worlds larger. The rest of the universe appears to succumb to the Empire's fearful reign rather than fight back against tyranny. However, one small band of Rebels, much like the early Christian church, believes that good still exists and that it is worth attacking the darkness to defend a cause. The early church believed in the reality of Christ and persevered despite the intolerance of the Roman world. For the Rebels, death is to be expected. For the early church, death and persecution were also to be expected. The chances of success for Christ's early church and for the Rebels were probably about equal. Translation: Would you be willing to be shot from point-blank range so that someone else could have the freedom to know about Jesus?

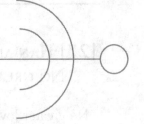

EPISODE V
THE EMPIRE STRIKES BACK

[26] HAN SOLO'S UNFINISHED BUSINESS.

At the start of the second movie, Han Solo helps get the sensors in place, then informs General Carlist Rieekan that he needs to settle some unfinished business with Jabba the Hutt. This is an example of the true statement that comes out in Numbers 32:23, "Be sure your sins will find you out." Han's dumping of cargo when smuggling for Jabba might not exactly be considered a sin, but his dealings with Jabba and his involvement in illegal smuggling clearly represents a sinful life, following a wrong path, and a path of dishonesty. This is Han's pre-conversion life, so to speak. Those things "done and left undone," as the Anglican liturgy puts it, can come back to haunt us. Taking care of them before they have a chance to catch up with us is a good course of action. It seems as if Han's past does almost come back to haunt him, as he tells Leia that the bounty hunter they run into in Ord Mantell "changed his mind."

Han's leaving is also an example of what Jesus said, "Give to Caesar what is Caesar's." If we owe someone money, or anything, it is good to repay it.

[27] HAN AND LUKE IN THE SNOW AND ICE OF HOTH. NO GREATER LOVE HAS A MAN THAN THIS. . . .

No greater love has a man than this, that he goes out into a sub-arctic night, freezes his ass off, and risks death by exposure to the cold to save his buddy. There is no hesitation in Han Solo about sacrificing his life to find Luke Skywalker.

> No greater love has a man than this, that he lay down his life for his friends.
>
> (John 15:13)

This verse was previously quoted in this book, but as this is a very Jedi verse, it bears repeating. It was not at all smart for Han to go out after Luke. Was there a smarter way? Could he not wait for morning when the speeders are ready? Not to second-guess the story, but this scene clearly shows us that Han thinks little of his own safety when his friends are in danger. It is surprising, and perhaps it is simply a story device, that no one else goes with him.

The western world bases its entire civilization on hard work and being smart, finding a better way to do things. It is an important ethic to have, but does the western world—Europe and America mostly—go too far with that notion to the detriment of dropping all cares about ourselves to save our friends? Our going immediately into Africa to stop the torture, the corruption, the violence, the genocide, the famine, or even the stifling of sub-Saharan Africa commerce would be examples of our nation behaving like Han Solo does in going out in the dead cold to find Luke.

[28] A YOUNG JEDI, NOT MINDFUL WHERE HE IS OR WHAT HE IS DOING, GETS MAULED BY A WAMPA ICE CREATURE.

Not that being mauled by a wampa ice creature, being hauled back to its cave, and getting hung upside down isn't enough to wreck someone's concentration, but a fully trained Jedi Knight likely could more easily sense the beast's presence and handle things differently. Luke is not yet fully trained, however, and he often cannot keep his bearings. He barely manages to escape when—after slicing off the wampa's arm—he runs out of the cave into a blizzard instead of killing the icy monster and staying protected in the cave until help arrives. This scene acts as part of the *before* in the before and after of Luke Skywalker's training. Luke's immaturity in *Episode IV: A New Hope* and again in his failure here, is an image of Luke learning about the Force, harnessing its energy, and controlling himself. Luke's development is unlike Neo's instant knowledge after downloading software in *The Matrix*. Luke is not suddenly a Jedi Knight simply for the wanting of it, or the implantation of software. Therefore, we see Luke develop, make mistakes, and almost die because of them.

People highly trained in spiritual matters have another trait that is very Jedi-like. Granted, this trait does not seem to have much to do with combating ice creatures. The metaphor at work here is that Luke's failure stems from a lack of spiritual training. We often equate a high level of spiritual training—this does not necessarily mean preachers or priests—with the ability to endure the things in life that normally wear down people socially, physically, or emotionally. You know how social interactions can easily derail through some small misunderstanding that someone exaggerates until it offends others in the relationship? Such things can easily knock us off balance emotionally and spiritually. Then there are those who are highly trained spiritually. Outwardly they do not appear to be any more spiritual than others. They are neither more mystical nor supernaturally magical than you or I. They are not easily offended, however. You leave their presence feeling liked, genuinely appreciated, and with a knowledge that he or she is personally interested. They seem to ask more questions rather than talk about themselves, and their words are rarely harsh or cutting.

Now, imagine that same person in a fender-bender accident. They don't immediately start yelling at the person who collided with their vehicle. They seem to take matters in stride. These people are quick to forget wrongs and even quicker to forgive. By contrast, it seems that other people who are less spiritually mature constantly endure problems that threaten their sanity, financial security, or friendships. These days, TV shows are full of these weak, snippy, over-reacting characters. Worse is when you see, hear, or experience a person who emulates those TV characters. This is very ugly behavior. A Jedi is calm, planning, generous, not over-reacting, never concerned about self. He does not say I, I, I in every sentence. Neither the Jedi nor the spiritually trained individual seem to have the same problems as everyone else, partly because they do not allow themselves to get into stupid situations and partly because they do not allow life's bumps and bruises to rule their emotions. They do not dwell on the bad things that come their way.

[29] LUKE'S VISION OF BEN KENOBI JUST BEFORE LUKE FAINTS IN THE BLIZZARD.

As Luke collapses in the blinding snowstorm, he has his first vision of post-death Obi-Wan Kenobi. Ben tells him to go to Dagobah to train with Yoda. Luke then faints in the blizzard.

You might liken this to hearing a voice in your head of some wise person who has passed away. What would they do in this situation, you might ask. Though in this specific example, Luke has never heard of Dagobah. This is not advice from Luke's short-lived knowledge of Ben's character. Instead, it is a specific direction from the spirit world. Ben's guidance is closer to hearing the Holy Spirit. Often the Holy Spirit gives us impressions, direction, guidance, or wisdom. Jesus refers to the Holy Spirit as Counselor. Ben Kenobi, as a symbol of the Holy Spirit, was in fact one of the original intentions (*Skywalking*, p. 145) that never made it to the filming stage.

Another very close metaphor of first Ben alone, then later Ben with Yoda and Anakin appearing as Force ghosts, is that of Christ's transfiguration. Although we do not know if Moses and Elijah appeared somehow in the flesh with Jesus, or merely as spirits, the imagery is still very much the same.

[30] DAGOBAH 1—
THE SIMPLE TO CONFUSE THE WISE.

Traditionally, Act I in a play is the hook, the first action where we meet the characters and establish our sympathies toward them. Act II is where the actors flesh out the author's belief system and where characters grow and change. Act III contains the drama's resolution, when the audience is fully committed to the play's hero or heroes, and the characters' growth enables them to defeat impossible odds.

Episode V: The Empire Strikes Back is a true second act in terms of the growth shown by all of the main characters, especially Luke. As a point of reference for those readers not entirely familiar with *Star Wars* (Hi, Mom!), the planet Dagobah is where Luke learns about what it is to be a Jedi Knight. This is where Yoda trains, tests, and mentors Luke.

Luke arrives at Yoda's hideaway by crashing his X-wing starfighter into a swamp. This failure to accomplish what should be a simple task foreshadows Luke's future and presents us with yet another metaphor for the messy state that is Luke's current development as a Jedi Knight. The fog thickens as Luke's X-wing approaches the planet's surface. The instruments of his technical world, on which he is depending on too heavily, finally stop working altogether. Luke's failure here is the opposite example from that of his using the Force to guide him in the Death Star's trench in the first movie. A Christian might describe Luke's actions on Dagobah as not living by faith. An even worse cliché might be, "Let go and let God." We hear these sentiments repeated often and without meaning. The idea behind all three, however, is very helpful. It is the constant realization that we are imperfect, that it is good and helpful for us to give up trying to control everything, and to continually remember to ask for God's help. In the *Star Wars* universe, this practice certainly would help Luke land his X-wing on Dagobah without incident, which he does do in *Episode VI: Return of the Jedi*, even though that landing is not shown. A distinctly Christian concept is that of *grace*, "the free and unmerited favor of God," according to the Oxford American Dictionary. Luke is successful when he understands that he is not able to accomplish the task of blowing up the Death Star by his own power. He needs the power of the Force. However, in this small, relatively common task of landing in the murky atmosphere of Dagobah, he forgets that lesson in humility.

Luke starts to set up camp and quickly meets Yoda.

It is not obvious to us whether Luke ever learns Yoda's first lesson about how the simple confuses the supposedly wise. However, in our first views of Yoda acting as a quirky creature, Yoda is trying to teach Luke something that is just as true for us. We often look to those beautiful people around us who seem successful, and think they must be wise. Luke certainly has his own notions of the outward appearance of a great warrior. In America, we go to gross extremes in the prevalent thinking that since sports and entertainment figures are celebrities, therefore, they must also be wise. When interviewed, reporters very often ask these celebrities probing questions about things well outside the interviewee's particular field of expertise, as if they must know more than we do simply because of their celebrity status. It is also tempting to mistake a politician in a tailored suit for being wise. In truth, the wise among us may very likely shy away from politics, may not seem as beautiful, as well groomed, or as physically fit as a finely-tailored person who wants your vote and who might easily do unwise things to obtain it. This is all to say that a tiny, green creature with pointed ears is usually not what one expects in a wise and powerful Jedi Knight. Yoda knows this and exaggerates it by acting even more strangely, on purpose, and not like a Jedi Master, to teach Luke not to judge by appearances.

[31] DAGOBAH 2—YODA'S FIRST LESSONS TO LUKE AND LUKE'S TESTING.

Before Luke even knows that he is in the presence of Yoda, Yoda brings him to his cave and makes dinner for him. This is what Jesus was like. Yoda serves Luke first just as Jesus washed the feet of his own disciples. If anything, student Luke should serve master Yoda. A second wisdom is the simple understanding that we all have physical needs. We must eat. Yoda would probably agree with a similar hierarchy to Maslow's of security, social, ego, and finally, spiritual needs.

Yoda is not quick to tell Luke who he is, and he does not seem anxious to start Luke's training. In Yoda's slowness, however, the training had already begun without Luke's knowing. This is another example of the Jedi concept of time from the fourth entry in this book. In the excerpts below, the fullness of time has come for Luke to be trained.

Yoda (before Luke knows him as such) – "Why wish you become a Jedi? Hm?"

Luke   –   "Mostly because of my father, I guess."

Yoda   –   "Ah, your father. Powerful Jedi was he, powerful Jedi, mmm."

Luke   –   "Oh, come on. How could you know my father? You don't even know who I am. Oh, I don't know what I'm doing here. We're wasting our time!"

Yoda (to the air) – "I cannot teach him. The boy has no patience."

Ben's voice –   "He will learn patience."

Yoda   –   "Hmmm. Much anger in him, like his father."

Ben's voice –   "Was I any different when you taught me?" Luke slowly realizes that this little, green creature is Yoda.

Yoda   –   "Hah. He is not ready."

Luke   –   "Yoda! I am ready. I . . . Ben! I can be a Jedi. Ben, tell him I'm ready."

Yoda   –   "Ready, are you? What know you of ready? For eight hundred years have I trained Jedi. My own council will I keep on who is to be trained! A Jedi must have the deepest commitment, the most serious mind. This one a long time have I watched. All his life has he looked away . . . to the future, to the horizon. Never his mind on where he was. Hmm? What he was doing . . . ."

Episode V: The Empire Strikes Back

On Tatooine, Luke is always looking away from where he is, eager to be on to bigger and better things, hoping that his future holds more than existence as a moisture farmer. It is good that he knows he wants to go to the Academy, and it is good that he wants to join the Rebellion. Luke looking to the sunset, longing for something better is good as long as he puts his mind to the present. But he allows his dreams and longings to distract him from the tasks at hand. Luke focuses on the stars, on the romantic ideas of success, of a new life, of an exciting life, of a celebrity's life. We are like this when we wish to have success without sacrifice. For example: never having written a book and yet overly imagining its publication instead of actually writing it. Yoda knows that Luke will not reach his goal because Luke is not focusing on how to get there. Without taking any steps, without doing well on what is right in front of him, Luke seeks success. Look how many people on TV want instant celebrity without having to work for it. This causes ugliness. Watch practically any reality TV show and you will see bad acting, bad singing, bad writing, etc. This is like the parable of the rich man's house built on the sand. Since there is no foundation, the storm easily sweeps away the house.

In his wisdom, Yoda is not saying something mysterious, nebulous or mythical; he is simply stating a fact. Unless you keep your mind on where you are—the next step in front of you—you will never reach your ultimate goal many more steps ahead. Think of most video games where the player must beat one level, or master certain skills, before moving on to harder levels and better skills. What would happen in most video games if you jumped to a level you were not ready for? The same goes for Luke on Dagobah, as it does for us in our physical and spiritual lives. First, master the level you're at, where you are, what you are doing.

[32] ADVENTURE. EXCITEMENT.
AN ACTION-ADVENTURE MOVIE CRAVES
NOT THESE THINGS . . .
WAIT . . . NO, MAYBE THEY DO.
THEN YODA TELLS LUKE TO BE AFRAID.
ISN'T FEAR FROM THE DARK SIDE?

Yoda   –   "Hmph. Adventure. Heh! Excitement. Heh! A Jedi craves not these things. You are reckless!"

Episode V: The Empire Strikes Back

On one level, this is an action-adventure film. As such, action and adventure are necessary. Luke's dreaming about a future life is all about his craving for action and adventure, and the first experiences he has with the Force are certainly in the context of high adventure and life-or-death realities. Now, this great warrior tells Luke that the Jedi life is not like that. It's like believing those glamorous U.S. Army commercials, then enlisting only to realize reality is anything but. Luke certainly has cause to wonder, and so would we if the film did not move so quickly into the next action sequence and series of special effects. We really do learn about the Force in those quiet moments sandwiched between the action shots. If *Star Wars* had been made in a different genre, or perhaps made as an indie, we might see deeper meaning in the smallness of life as a Jedi exists between times of action. We might better understand how these times are also important. Or is it simply true that if we remain still, action will gravitate to us?

Ben's voice –   "So was I, if you'll remember."
Yoda   –   "He is too old. Yes, too old to begin the training."
Luke   –   "But I've learned so much."
Yoda   –   "Will he finish what he begins?"
Luke   –   "I won't fail you. I'm not afraid."
Yoda   –   "Then, you will be. You will be!"

Episode V: The Empire Strikes Back

As we learn in the next few scenes, Yoda teaches Luke that anger, fear, and aggression lead to the dark side. Is Yoda saying that the dark side is good? No, not at all. The subtle distinction is that Yoda is talking about Luke having a healthy apprehension for the power of the Force. There are similarities between the Force and the true God, and to this end, this statement of Yoda's means something even deeper. When he says, "Then, you will be [afraid]," this is like,

> The fear of the Lord is the beginning of wisdom; all who follow his precepts have good understanding. To him belongs eternal praise.
>
> (Psalm 111:10)

We must fear God, and obey him. The fear of God leads to love, which involves letting go of ourselves, as we will see shortly. This is not the same fear that leads to the dark side. The fear that leads to the dark side happens when we allow our fear to overwhelm us.

> Do not be afraid of those who kill the body but cannot kill the soul. Rather, be afraid of the One who can destroy both soul and body in hell.
>
> (Matthew 10:28)

The dark side breeds the opposite of peace through overwhelming fear for ourselves, our bodies, our possessions, our feelings. It makes us anxious to hold on to those things instead of letting go of them.

[33] DAGOBAH 3—A JEDI'S STRENGTH
FLOWS FROM THE FORCE.

Scene: As Luke runs around a dark, swampy, Dagobah fitness course, Yoda holds onto his back and teaches him about the Force.

Yoda — "Run! Yes. A Jedi's strength flows from the Force. But beware of the dark side. Anger . . . fear . . . aggression. The dark side of the Force are they. Easily they flow, quick to join you in a fight. If once you start down the dark path, forever will it dominate your destiny, consume you it will, as it did Obi-Wan's apprentice."

Luke — "Vader? Is the dark side stronger?"

Yoda — "No . . . no . . . no. Quicker, easier, more seductive."

Luke — "But how am I to know the good side from the bad?"

Yoda — "You will know. When you are calm, at peace. Passive. A Jedi uses the Force for knowledge and defense, never for attack."

Luke — "But tell me why I can't . . ."

Yoda — "No, no, there is no why. Nothing more will I teach you today. Clear your mind of questions. Mmm. Mmmmmmmmm."

Episode V: The Empire Strikes Back

Yoda presents Luke with this idea that there is this energy—this power—that is at the same time both good and bad. Yoda cautions Luke not to use the bad part of this energy. It is more than a little confusing that the whole Force flows, but that one part is accepted while the other part is blocked and rejected. Future entries will address this confusing topic. It is important to focus first on the yes, which is to explore that which is true about Yoda's teachings.

Once you start down the dark path,
forever will it dominate your destiny.

As long as man has counted time, even down to daily life, history echoes this truth: The darkest ages in the history of the world are hallmarked by anger, fear, and aggression. Lies and deception are also hallmarks of the dark side, and we see this in greater detail in the movie prequels. If we decide to cheat, lie, steal, etc., or if we decide to allow fear of things or people to motivate us, then we start slipping over to the dark side.

Our world is not black and white, though. Sometimes we are caught believing something is right when it is neither right nor good. We are often deceived into doing something or thinking something. How is a businessman to know whether his practices are counterproductive to society and ultimately to himself? How is a lawyer to know when more laws negatively affect life and freedom? Granted, there are those who choose to enrich themselves to the extreme detriment of others. There are a great many more of us who get mired in the issues that are not clearly black and white, or have a hard time knowing what course of action is the wisest. One thing many Christians have a hard time dealing with is Roe v. Wade—the Supreme Court ruling that, whether intended or not, brought about abortion on demand. Many Christians have a difficult time believing that people who support abortion are not monsters; and they certainly have a hard time even imagining that these people are trying to do something that is good. Those who support abortion often have the same limitations of perspective in reverse. So what do we do? The few successful debates on the issue I have seen have started with both parties being individually calm, at peace.

When you are calm, at peace

Yoda's direction is helpful because of its truth. To know the difference between light and dark, one must practice being calm, peaceful, and passive. When we find ourselves caught up in the details of life, the hot and important issues, the rushing around, the busyness of daily life, how often do we lose focus and forget why it is that we are so busy in the first place? What does the bustling about do for us, anyway? What do we accomplish by showing anger to each other in hotly contested debates? In this book's introduction, I mentioned that this concept can be used for more than just helping to distinguish good from evil, and keeping one from making decisions while angry. The practice of being calm and at peace is vital to maintaining a cool mind and a warm heart if we are ever to seriously deal with the abortion issue, and a multitude of other issues that do not seem clear to us because we are in the middle of too many other things. Failure to maintain a cool mind and a warm heart leaves us weak, possibly worthless, for the fights that we need to fight. Think of monks, and how they practice being quiet, even to the point of taking vows of silence. They meditate and are thoughtful. They slow down and are attentive to every movement of their bodies. The Jedi are like this, and this peacefulness helps them to focus in times of action.

The Tao concept from which Lucas draws this is the virtue of contentment. My definition of contentment is a conscious practice of naming those things that God has given to me, both material and immaterial, and thanking him for each one individually. After I do this, I realize that God is providing for me and that I lack nothing. This may seem to be a side track from the heated issues of our day, or more like the philosophy of getting done what we have to do today. Peace, however, starts with us as individuals. Operating from a peaceful center is the Jedi way. Therefore, I thank God for a bed, for a blessed family, for safety, for his coming to me and being with me, for a car, for food. On and on I go. Obviously God did not pop out of the sky and deposit these things on my doorstep. I am also involved in the process and can be wise with my time, money, relationships, etc., or I can act foolishly and, most likely, lose those gifts. The purpose of getting to a state of contentment is to be thankful to the God who made all things possible, who gives life. This practice resets what we expect out of life.

The idea of peace includes being content, and then goes even farther. Peace is quiet satisfaction in the practice of faith. It is feeling restful in good times and bad, having confidence that God is in control of things even when we do not feel provided for, and even up to the point of understanding that in our death and what lies beyond he is right with us, bringing us home. This is not easy. Peace is not natural to our sinful state. It is a gift of God's Holy Spirit to be used and practiced. It is an internal and an external condition that allows the growth of our spirit.

How do we get to that peaceful place? Jesus was the example of, "slow to anger, abounding in love." Often Jesus would give people peace, sometimes just by being peaceful, sometimes by saying, "Peace." However, he was God—sinless and perfect—so how do we get there?

Here is how we do it.

> Rejoice in the Lord always. I will say it again: Rejoice! Let your gentleness be evident to all. The Lord is near. Do not be anxious about anything, but in everything, by prayer and petition, with thanksgiving, present your requests to God. And the peace of God which transcends all understanding, will guard your hearts and your minds in Christ Jesus.
>
> (Philippians 4:4–7)

Translation: When you have a hard time getting to a peaceful place inside you, sing and lift your hands up to the being who made you, who loves you, and who wants to commune with you—the trinity God. Praise him, as in tell him all the good things he is. Be gentle in your movements. Then, don't freak out about stuff. Instead, when you start getting uptight, tell God about it and ask him to take those emotions away. Even though this might seem impossible, he will bring you peace if you seek his help. He will do this through the Holy Spirit working in you. It also helps to know what Jesus said while he was on earth, and what he led his apostles to say about him. This is so vitally important. Even people who know Jesus have a hard time not being anxious.

Once we are at peace, we will be able to see our path clearly.

Knowledge and Defense

Yoda said that the Jedi use the Force for knowledge and defense only. Yoda links this to their ability to be at peace. When the Jedi are mindful of the Force, the situations they enter into seem to be led or predestined. There seems to be a natural flow to their movements, to where they go, and to what they find out on their missions. This knowledge is portrayed as partly psychic-intuitive, and partly in knowing how to control themselves. Anger, fear, and aggression lead to controlling others. The Jedi seek to control only themselves. Not to be overly Pollyanna about this, but if you ever try breathing slowly and deeply, blocking out all the issues that are crowding you out, focusing on the next step, life does fall into place a little better. This practice of meditation is important to Buddhists, and it is a very practical one for anyone else as well.

We are able to determine our destiny to a certain extent, and these practices help us to know how. This is using the Force for knowledge because in this frame of mind we are better able to see a correct view of ourselves and the world. If breathing and being mindful work for you, add worshipping God to this practice. The New Testament story of Paul and Silas in prison is a good example in this context. They are in jail, physically beaten, and with full justification to be angry at life, at the Romans, at the Jews, and at God for things that are not going their way. Instead of moping, however, they sing praises to God. This story presents to us an example of maturity and wisdom under pressure. The Force is with Paul and Silas even when their mission and their lives are not going successfully by anyone's standards. Their attitudes defend them against despair, anger, fear—the dark side. This is how to use the Force for defense, and it will not likely make much sense until you try it.

Clear your mind of questions

Finally, in this excerpt, Yoda says, "Clear your mind of questions." Certainly, he is not saying that Luke should never ask questions. In fact, this is the only way that Luke has learned anything thus far, the good old Socratic method of question and answer. Yoda is saying, however, that there is a time when our minds get wound up. When this happens, it is time to rest and consider what we have already learned for a while instead of going forward with further training.

How many drugs are on the market today to reduce anxiety and induce peace largely due to our failure to practice the teachings of Yoda?

[34] DAGOBAH 4—THE LIGHT SIDE/DARK SIDE AND HOW GEORGE LUCAS IS LIKE GOD.

It is time to address this light side/dark side concept in *Star Wars*. *Star Wars* espouses a philosophy that there is a bad and good side to the energy that all living things create and that binds the universe together. This has the appearance of Taoist philosophy. However, it is only the appearance, mind you. It is important to note that the following pages will comment on the philosophy of *Star Wars* as the movies present it. Although there are clear, intentional similarities to Taoism and to other belief systems in *Star Wars*, these likenesses are not presented as those belief systems themselves. Obviously, the Jedi religion, the Sith religion, and the ways of the Force belong to the fictional myth stories of the *Star Wars* series. To this extent, they are not real. However, myths lie at the core of humanity's belief systems, and because *Star Wars* is a mythic tale there will be connections that we see and feel simply from the nature of this type of story. To this extent, the ideas in *Star Wars* are therefore very real.

Any notion that *Star Wars* actually shows us a world in which good and evil derive from the same source needs to be rejected outright. To the contrary, the Force is never shown to us in a context outside of the people who use it. This is to say that we only see the Force as a superpower that is utilized for good or for evil within the actions and speech of individual characters. As such, the Force can be said to have an amazing likeness to the utilization of God's image in us, which is the subject of entries 7 and 35. The description of the Force as good and evil and part of the same life-energy is not only an unsustainable concept, it is also not supported by the *Star Wars* universe. There is a crucial distinction between the life-energy being good and evil, and aspects of life-energy being used for good or evil within a person.

The concern I have is that people who love *Star Wars* will just accept that the Force is like God, and start thinking that God is both good and bad. In fact, George Lucas wanted to illustrate this point in the film series. For Lucas, the Force in *Star Wars* means that things will go better for you if you choose to follow God's light side—the good, instead of his dark side—the evil.[7]

The first problem with this concept is that if choosing the light side or the dark side are both OK, and that the light side simply works out better, then choosing the dark side is also a valid choice. And though it may be a path that does not function as well as choosing the light side there is nothing inherently pejorative, negative, or erroneous about choosing the dark side. Lucas may believe that God is both good and evil, but this philosophy is not supported anywhere in the *Star Wars* universe, or in ours either for that matter. In *Star Wars*, Lucas portrays the dark side as completely lacking in value, which could not be true if it was simply another aspect of God's dual nature. The second problem in associating God with both good and evil is this: if a being is both good and evil, that being cannot be God. If a being exists that created the universe and is eternal, he must be love, and love cannot, by definition, be evil. His creating would be offset by his destroying, his love by his hate. We would know love and hate as fickle elements that are neither to be trusted. This is not true in our universe, and it is most certainly not true in the *Star Wars* universe that Lucas has masterfully created for us.

Indeed, we see the reflection of Lucas the creator throughout *Star Wars*: his love is by no means fickle or intransigent—he loves his creations, both the good and the evil. Does he love the characters because they are evil, or despite their evil behavior? In other words, does Lucas want Vader to be evil? In her book, *The Mind of the Maker*, Dorothy Sayers shows us that we know something of who God is based on what we know about the stories we write, and about our relationships with our own characters. We can understand a small portion of how God must relate to us by how we relate to the literary characters of our own creation. Using this approach we can ask, does Lucas find it good that some of his creations do evil things? Do they act in spite of their maker's love or do the evil characters just do what they are supposed to, what Lucas makes them do? If Darth Vader, for example, kills people mercilessly because he is supposed to be evil, and this is just the role he is to play, there would be a resignation in his character that he has no choice in the matter, but must simply follow the orders of his creator (Lucas). Evil would not really even be evil. Darth Vader would not mercilessly kill because he is acting against something, because he chose this route of his own free will. Evil would instead be a lackluster, "I'm doing this because I am the bad guy character and am forced to behave this way." The terror is taken out of Darth Vader and every other Sith if they don't act as free characters who decide to be evil. We would rather have sympathy for the unfortunate position they find themselves in. We would then be led to think the only evil is really with the Creator, who made them be like this. Bad, bad Creator.

This is not the world we know. Darth Vader is evil because he chooses to be. There is a tension between the creator Lucas and his creation, Vader, because Anakin/Vader in *Episode II: Attack of the Clones* starts to go down the wrong path. The way the movies are made cause us to grieve for his decline. Nowhere do we see that it is OK for him to become evil. The same applies to characters with whom we are not as invested. It is clear to us that the seedy and evil characters are not what they could be, their evil natures cause them to be lesser than their potential. In *Episode II: Attack of the Clones*, Count Dooku has fallen from the position of Jedi Knight. Palpatine would have made a great leader and would have been a better good guy than bad guy. Even at the end of *Episode VI: Return of the Jedi*, when Vader turns back to good, Vader is not meekly asking permission from his creator to please play a good guy now. Vader is a real character because he actually chooses to turn his life around, pursue love, and save his son, even though he forfeits his life. We all know that Vader chooses to return to the good side, and it is hardly believable that George Lucas would be passionless about this. Instead, the beauty of that scene seems to show that he and the other filmmakers, along with millions of the rest of us, feel relief that we are witnessing the salvation of a soul. It is the nature of our universe that in order to create a good story, a true and real story, we must allow characters to be good or evil. Allowing characters to choose is one way we express our own image in them, our gift of life to them. The more we are able to do this, the more real our characters become to the reader. As with all story tellers, Lucas still creates and tells the story. But if his characters had no autonomy, then his stories would be wooden, lifeless. He would be a merciless creator who demands that his characters play out their predestined mechanical roles. Obviously this is not what happens in *Star Wars*. And this is not what happens to us when God allows us to do what we will.

[35] THE LIGHT AND DARK SIDE IN ALL OF US. HOW WE USE THE FORCE OF GOD'S IMAGE.

All the *Star Wars* movies describe the dark and light side of the Force within the context of people. It is within this context that I see the best translation of the Force into our own world.

If the Bible is correct, God is not good and evil, he is all good, and he has created mankind in his image. God's image within us means that we are his most special creation on this planet. There are many qualities to being God's most special creation on Earth that set us apart from every other creation on this planet. The fact that we can do anything we like with his image in us is like the Force having a dark side and a light side. We can use God's image in us to do good things or evil things, just as we saw in the example of Vader's free will in the last entry. We can also use this Force to create things, then use those things for good or evil. Nuclear power is the most dramatic example of mankind's ability to create and use a creation for good and evil.

In choosing evil, we are even using this Force to un-choose the one who gave us the ability to choose. If God were to take away our ability to choose, he would be removing his image from within us; it would be taking our humanity away from us. Can you imagine Lucas not allowing Anakin to turn to evil? He would cease to be Anakin. God allows us to use the Force that he gave us—his image—for good or for evil, to follow him or not. He allows us to take our own humanity away from ourselves. Because his image is a special gift, it comes with a special price; God judges us on how we use the Force he gives us. Have we become powerful in the Force or have we used it for nothing? The Force he gives us is like the parable of the talents. If we hide the abilities he has given us in the ground, so to speak, he will judge us harshly for this waste. He judges us even more harshly for using the Force for evil.

God's image in us has made us able to create abilities, skills, technologies, economies, cultures, art, and scientific discoveries. Yet, within the magnificent creation that is our bodies and our minds, and the worlds we make with them, we cannot even control ourselves.

We cannot prevent ourselves, as individuals or as a community, from doing things we do not want to do. There is no such thing as a master race that has evolved past this point. Whenever a group of humanity thinks itself nearing perfection, it always finds itself on the brink of evil, rotting from the inside. We cannot even eradicate pain, poverty, or hunger!

The Force is a good way to understand the power of God's image in us. We can create great works and deeds without even believing in God. In fact, we can do great things and be actively working against God. By becoming more of a person, enhancing our skills, etc., we increase the power of our image just as a Jedi or a Sith trains. We increase our ability to do more and be more. The more we do towards the good, the harder it is for us to quickly turn and be bad. Mother Theresa had great power in her service of others, and her ability to be selfless is legendary. Hitler had great power of persuasion, a great ability to turn people against other people, and a great ability to hurt people without caring. Mother Theresa had a great ability to love, Hitler had a great ability to hate. A Hitler would not turn around and magically become a Mother Theresa, but his image—his person—had great power just as she had. This is like the choosing of the light side and dark side—we can choose a path and go far down it. We can also choose to not go far down a path at all.

Think about humans that stay very low in their image. These people rarely have a desire to do much of anything, good or bad. We commonly call this ignorance. We are all afflicted with this to some extent, but it seems that the more aware we are of our ignorance, and the more we seek not to be ignorant, the greater our image becomes. This does not mean our soul is any better or worse than another's. There is simply a separation between what we are able to do. Do you know how to be a doctor, a lawyer, a scientist, or a helper? What do we do with who we are? Towards what end do we doctor, lawyer, or help? The Force is like the knowledge, skills, and abilities that exist in the world that we can learn about and possess within ourselves. How we use the Force is our personality, our will, choosing and pushing ourselves to the light side or the dark side.

An odd quality of being made in God's image and yet not bound to be him or be like him is that it is possible for us to use the power of hate. We can devolve or un-become. Our history is by no means a gradual state of getting better and better. There are dark times that set us back, that kill innocent people. All major civilizations have problems that threaten to undo that which made them great. It is also possible for us to be not as smart, not as wise, not as healthy, not as good a person as our father or our mother. It is possible for us to destroy something good.

[36] THE JEDI PURSUIT OF HAPPINESS AND THE FOLLY OF POLITICAL CORRECTNESS.

> Whatever is true, whatever is noble, whatever is right, whatever is pure, whatever is lovely, whatever is admirable—if anything is excellent or praiseworthy—think about such things.
>
> (Philippians 4:8)

In the United States of America, one of our constitutionally-guaranteed freedoms is the pursuit of happiness. The tricky thing is that the concept of happiness can lead some people to greed, lust, and all manner of bad things. Happiness can be very arbitrary. In order for one person to be happy, they may be very comfortable even if it causes someone else to be unhappy. Worse, they—we—may not care enough to even be aware of the situation. We like inexpensive clothes, but we often don't realize someone's basic human rights were violated in the making of them. How many items from China do each of us own, for example? Some people say that China is coming along, and well it may be. However, even the poorest person in America would refuse to work under the conditions that many factory workers must in China. If you were a Chinese factory worker and someone treated you unfairly, what would you do? Every person who buys such merchandise is partially responsible for supporting those conditions. It may be bad for a Chinese worker's health to work in those places, but what kind of a toll does it take on the souls of those who enable those deplorable conditions to continue?

Not that we particularly have any direct words on this subject from a Jedi, but it is not far fetched to take the selfless character of the Jedi and suggest that it might be wiser if the words of our Constitution read, "pursuit of joy." The word *joy* requires a stricter moral code than does the word *happiness. Joy* means we don't always have to feel effervescently giddy about our life situation. It means we feel better when we place another's happiness before our own. It means that things do not always have to go our way for us to act magnanimous. It means more and bigger are not necessarily better.

The second downfall in our pursuit of happiness, as it seems to be misinterpreted today, is that there is a common assumption that everyone should possess this happiness. This is similar to thinking that all of us are fit to be Jedi, which is a great and stupid idea. The Jedi had a rigorous training program in addition to the fact that the Force is stronger in certain people than it is in others. When Luke tells Leia in *Episode VI: Return of the Jedi* that she is his sister, this becomes part of his explanation that the Force is strong in his family. Leia has more of an aptitude for using the Force than Han, for example. In *Episode I: The Phantom Menace*, Ani is tested for his midiclorian level and we learn that all children are tested for this in the Republic, and identified early for this honor (thought this starts to sound communistic to me). The amount of these organisms inside a person supposedly determines their ability to use the Force. Some people were not strong enough to become Jedi, and some Jedi became stronger than others. As much as believers in political correctness may hate to hear this, individuals are limited in our world, too. Some of us do not have the mental capacity for certain disciplines, either through natural or socialized limitations, or through natural or socialized inheritance.

To be fair, those who believe in political correctness do have an extremely good point in that humanity is hardly at the point where we can even know an individual's limitations, so we need to give people as many opportunities as possible to succeed. The Republic in *Star Wars* may have been closer to this goal than we are. Socioeconomic and cultural inequalities leave many of us with much less of a chance to pursue happiness than a Caucasian country-clubber.

Enter in the eternal paradox of Jesus.

Eternally speaking, is working in a Chinese factory or not growing up as a member of a white family with old money all that much of a disadvantage? In *Star Wars* terms, are we really all that disadvantaged by not being a Luke Skywalker?

Fighting the evil and the wrong in this world is the right thing to do. There are egregious errors in our world today. We must work diligently to help the world's poorest millions and battle the political systems that put them there, along with those others that keep them there. Thinking long term, though, Jesus more than levels the playing field. In fact, it may be much harder for that Caucasian country-clubber to enter the kingdom of heaven—think of a camel trying to crawl through a very small door. So would you rather have wealth and privilege for 80 or 90 years and then end up with eternal nothing? Or would you rather be a factory worker in China for roughly the same number of years and end up a king for eternity and personally know the Creator? Granted, life is not exactly that extreme for the vast majority of us. The lesson is the same, however. Money and power and fame—all extremes of the pursuit of happiness in this life concept, threaten to take us away from knowing God, which for the sake of the metaphor could be seen as happiness forever. However many years you have lived will seem like less than half of a half of a half of a percent the minute after you die. The only part of that infinitesimally short experience that matters will be who you became during that moment. Who you became in an eternal perspective means what was the quality of your love to other people? Did you use the Force inside you—however much of it you could develop—to sustain and encourage life? Finally, did you acknowledge Jesus as the one who saves you from the dark path?

The Jedi pursuit of happiness does not revolve around material wealth, individual power, or professional success. The Jedi seem to find joy in not being encumbered by possessions, by the giving of their great power to the least powerful, and by measuring success in terms of giving rather than receiving, in the good of all versus the good of one. This behavior is strangely Christ-like.

[37] Balancing what appears to be contradictory in the light side and the dark side of the Force. As in, what is right about the light and dark sides being one.

The core idea of Tao—which is where Tai Chi comes from—is that nature exists in fields of opposites.[8] (*Star Wars and Philosophy*, Robinson, p. 31) This is a very important observation. Opposites do exist in nature and they do tug at each other, they do yin and yang, push and pull, *Sturm und Drang*. The emblem of Tai Chi, with the white swirl and the black swirl chasing each other inside a larger circle and a dot of the opposite color in the center of each swirl, is a great symbol. Rightly seen, it is a picture of balance, of tension between two ideas that seem contradictory, which is also a paradox. Let's look at examples from our everyday world, then see how *Star Wars* represents them.

Anyone who has lived on this planet for any length of time has experienced the opposite nature of male and female. We are man and we are woman. It is not true to say, though, that part of our opposite does not exist in ourselves. Masculine and feminine forces inside of us long for balance, and these are inextricably hooked to our gender. Balance, in this context, is not numerical or percentage-based, and does not result in androgyny. If the black swirl represents masculinity, there is a white dot of femininity inside it, and vice versa. A man is more of a man when he does not suppress the part of his being that is feminine. A woman is more of a woman when she does not suppress the masculine in herself. A healthy balance of these two opposing forces—masculine action and feminine beauty—results in a healthy person, and this is to be cultivated and encouraged in each other. Without a dot of the opposite trait to provide tension and balance, we cut ourselves off from nature. We end up in an unnatural state. If there exists only the black swirl of masculinity, that person ends up either hating and denying anything feminine, or becomes disgusted with the masculine-only view and embraces the feminine in an attempt to deny the masculine. Conversely, if there is only the white swirl of femininity, that person ends up either hating or denying anything masculine, or becomes disgusted with this feminine-only view and embraces the masculine in an attempt to deny the feminine. The same occurs when one has more than just a dot of the opposite. In balance, the white dot in no way makes a man into a woman, and the black dot in no way makes a woman into a man. For me, this points to God as creator of the Force, because there is no way that we can ever achieve balance between masculinity and femininity on our own. We are broken because of our nature and because of our nurture—i.e. social influences. The circle cannot hold together on its own power. God is on the outside holding the circle together, helping us be whole.

Another traditional Christian struggle between opposites is God's predestination versus man's free will. The Bible indicates that both are true, but it seems logical at first that these concepts must contradict each other. How can God cause things to happen *and* allow us to cause things to happen? Any attempt to comprehend this might blow a fuse in our brains. To accept that both do exist fully—although we are not entirely sure how—is to exercise faith, which is the tension of a paradox. In this example, one side is the white yin and one side is the dark yang. Again, any balance that we might attempt can only happen through God's doing; we have no idea how these two can both be true and yet co-exist.

Life and death is another excellent example of paradox, a Christian believes. Life—in our bodies and presumably on this planet—and death of our earthly bodies are both undeniable parts of existence as we know it. The circle surrounding the white and black swirls represents the truth of the existence of our soul. Perhaps the swirls demonstrate the natural cycle of our history, we live then we die, then the next generations live and die. We never live without dying and yet even after our bodies die our souls still live. How does this work? Faith is the tension of believing that bodily death, though unknown, is part of our existence, not the end of it. Of course the bummer is that, according to the Bible, if you don't confess your sins and believe in Christ, you don't get the black swirl.

So where do we see this balance, this tension in the *Star Wars* movies? Primarily we see it in the life of the Jedi. They have the power to control things and people, yet seek to control themselves and work to allow others to have more freedom. There is a balance of a Jedi's living in the present and being mindful of the future. Yoda on Dagobah teaches Luke spiritual truths about the Force at the same time that he trains Luke physically. A Jedi Knight is a warrior and a monk. The Jedi use technology and yet defer to the Force. They seek to use the Force for good, yet understand its misuse leads to evil. These are but a few of the yin yang paradoxes that exist in *Star Wars*.

Finally, what about the Force itself? It is definitely paradoxical, yet nonetheless very true, to say that balance keeps the tension between seeming opposites, lack of balance destroys it. In this way, Christians and Taoists have much agreement. The Jedi maintain balance of opposites which strengthens the Force's influence in themselves and in the world, whereas the Sith seek to destroy the balance and, ironically, the very source of power they claim to use. As you might surmise, this line of thought can only lead to questioning how the dark and the light can actually be part of one power, because good and evil certainly seem to be described in *Star Wars* as coming from the same Force. This is the subject of the next entry.

[38] What is wrong with the light and dark being one? Sin, entropy, and the divine Force: the duality of the Force.

This entry contains three subentries: Why the dark and the light sides of the Force cannot be part of one power. Why neither the Jedi nor the Sith are, or can be, one with the Force. Finally, Why the Force cannot be divine.

Why the dark and light sides of the Force cannot be part of one power.

Here is the core problem with the whole oneness of the Force thing: the Taoist idea of two opposing fields of nature, whose existence and tension fuel life, so to speak, are integrated with a Christian value system. The Force combines Taoism, which says these opposing fields of nature are only relative to each other, with the Christian belief that everything is relative to God—think holiness, love, the golden standard of goodness. The result of this mixture is good and evil that supposedly emanate from the same Force. This does not fit the teachings of either philosophy and does not make sense, even in the *Star Wars* universe.

For one, Taoism does not believe in absolute good and evil; it says they are relative to each other. The emblem of Tai Chi—the yin/yang symbol—is a limited but good visual representation of faith's paradox. Good and evil do not fit into this symbol, however. It might be more precise to use the terms holy and evil, or good and bad. Even so, these terms do not fit into the paradigm of a paradox since they are absolutes. Even though our language tends to treat them as opposites, this is not accurate. Taking holiness or goodness to its fullest sense results in God. Complete holiness is fully balanced, and he has no evil in him (1 John 1:5).

An interesting side note here: When Jesus said, "I am the way, the truth and the life. No man comes to the Father except through me,"

(John 14:6) it seems like an almost Taoist description of God, even though Taoists do not believe in God.

Complete evil or badness—Satan—is also fully unbalanced. There is, however, no equivalency. Since God created the Angel of Light— also known as Lucifer—it is not really even accurate to speak of Lucifer and God in opposing terms because God is complete and absolutely powerful and Satan is not. The creation is, by nature, not as powerful as the Creator. Therefore, it would be incorrect to try to strike a balance between good and evil. Though it is tempting to think that the commonality between the Force and Taoism promotes this dualism, it is unfounded. Evil is a taking away, a subtraction, a bite out of the circle represented by the emblem of Tai Chi. Evil seeks the extreme—think of the Sith—where there is no tension of opposites, a partial life circle and then ultimately no circle. Evil is not a correct interpretation of the black swirl in the context of white being the good swirl. In *Star Wars*, we see neither a tension nor a balancing of good and evil. Yoda and Palpatine never seek to coordinate their efforts.

In fact, why is Yoda the picture of the balance of the Force if he does not practice the dark side? Why don't we see Yoda in as unfavorable a light as Palpatine, the Sith Lord? Both are completely devoted—Yoda to the light, Palatine to the dark. Neither seeks to balance dark with light, good with evil.

Those who believe in the dark side practice control of others, i.e. deception, murder, hate, selfishness. Those who believe in the light side practice control of self, i.e. love, selflessness. The light side results in what the Bible calls "the fruit of the Spirit," or what the *Star Wars* universe might explain as the evidence that a person serves the light side: Love, joy, peace, patience, kindness, goodness, faithfulness, gentleness and self-control. No Jedi Knight is ever encouraged to learn about the dark side of the Force. No Sith is ever encouraged to use the light side of the Force. Instead, the *Star Wars* universe is always a moral universe where there are people who choose to be good and others who choose to be bad.

There is only one person in all six movies who tries to contain the light side and the dark side of the Force at the same time. This is

Anakin Skywalker as he is being deceived by the Emperor and the dark side in episodes II and III. This Lucas presents to us as an extremely bad thing. Anakin commits terrible atrocities. He struggles and eventually loses his sanity during the final climax when he fully devolves into Darth Vader. No man can serve two masters.

Finally, if evil is part of the Force—or part of God—the Jedi who choose good over evil would then be better than the Force. Similarly, such a decision on our part would make us better than God, which is hardly a real concept of either the all-powerful Force or the one true God who calls himself love. Thus, the words that describe the Force as both good and evil are either misleading, or do not represent a metaphor for God.

It is obvious that the makers of *Star Wars* want us to see a world in which good is the only OK option.

Why neither the Jedi nor the Sith are, or can be, completely one with the Force.

The primary reasons why the Jedi and the Sith cannot be fully one with the Force are sin and entropy.

Let's take sin first. Not only are absolute good and evil very real concepts in *Star Wars*, but the truth of Christ's teaching about sin is evidenced even in the trespasses of the Jedi. Characters in *Star Wars* struggle with sin just as we do on Earth. Sin is not mentioned outright, however it is possible for a Jedi to violate a religious, moral or ethical code, which is one definition of sin. It is also possible to transgress an agreed-upon set of rules, another definition of sin. Yoda teaches Luke that pursuing the dark side is wrong and that its path leads to that which is completely undesirable. It is shown as a negative thing in *Episode V: The Empire Strikes Back* that Luke's disobedience of Yoda in taking his weapons with him into the cave results in his using the Force out of aggression. Luke again disobeys Yoda and Obi-Wan's council when he falls into Vader's trap by traveling to Bespin, the Cloud City, to rescue his friends. Luke's transgression does not rescue his friends. In fact, it makes matters much worse and almost ends Luke's life. It is grace on many levels that

Vader only cut off Luke's right hand. Obi-Wan expresses lament in *Episode III: Revenge of the Sith* for being too hard on Anakin. And how about the whole point of all three prequels? Anakin, as a boy, is full of light, power, and selflessness. However, his decline to the dark side involves the sins of murder, lies, deceit and going against all religious, moral, ethical, and agreed-upon rules. If dark and light are one and a Jedi is able to merge and mould into it, he would come to see that doing something wrong, bad, or even incorrect did not exist. Such is not the experience or the thoughts of any Jedi in the entire series.

Whenever the Jedi violate religious, moral, and ethical codes, even if they transgress the agreed-upon set of rules, the result is a limitation of the ability to use the Force. Power flows more easily to the Sith because it is a fact of life that it is easier to be bad than good, to put yourself ahead of others. However, even the Sith face similar issues in that if they do something good or selfless, they act against the power they serve and this diminishes their abilities as well. Darth Vader is not his usual evil self in dealing with Princess Leia in *Episode IV: A New Hope*. Again, in *Episode V: The Empire Strikes Back*, Vader demonstrated Sith weakness by showing grace to Luke when Vader does not kill him. There are those fans who might disagree here and point out that Vader did tell the Emperor, "He will join us or die," so one might see Vader's efforts here as simply attempting to coax Luke to join him. One might also point out that Vader knows the rule of two—one Sith master, one Sith apprentice—and would likely expect a promotion if he can recruit Luke, but I remain unconvinced that Vader shows no affection for his son, Luke.

In our world, sin is proof that we are not one with God. This is an important topic because God and the Force are so often seen as similar. Because of sin, we—like the apostle Paul—do things we don't want to do (Romans 7). However, sin is more than just doing something we don't want to do. Our sin broke, and breaks, harmony with God. "The wages of sin is death . . . ." (Romans 6:23). Adam and Eve's original sin, as well as our continuing sin, caused and causes death to enter the process of nature, of which we are inextricably a part. Sin separates us from God, and is proof in itself that we are not God, nor can we ever be. The Bible also says that Jesus is the only one who ever lived who did not sin. So, unless you are Jesus, you can't be God. Them's the rules—sorry, Mormons.

So where does sin leave nature? Before man sinned in the Garden of Eden, describing nature as having a harmonious balance was exactly right. The Bible presents a world view that death was not originally part of the experience of life. To me, this seems much more harmonious and balanced than death being part of the experience of life and nature. The excellent emblem of Tai Chi, then, a good and simple description of the processes of the natural world in which we live, must therefore be separated from its description as "The Great Harmony" because a greater harmony did exist. After all, death is just not very harmonious or balanced.

This brings us to entropy. Original sin created entropy in that it destroyed the perfect balance of life, allowing death to enter the picture. Entropy is the tendency of all things towards disorder or chaos. More precisely, my Oxford American Dictionary explains it as, "the unavailability of a system's thermal energy for conversion into mechanical work, often interpreted as the degree of disorder or randomness in a system." The degree of randomness or disorder in a system seems like the process of life to death and back. If a tree takes life out of the ground, dies, and eventually returns its energy to the earth—isn't a lot of energy unavailable in the dying process? Perhaps a "system's thermal energy is unavailable" because the processes of life to death and death to life are disorderly, unbalanced, and requires the spending of energy in the process that could otherwise be used for mechanical work. Once life—a tree, in this example—is built back up, a system's energy is once again available. Wouldn't it be more harmonious if a system's energy did not tend toward death or disorder, but remained orderly and self-renewed without the process of death? Will Christ's return restore these processes? These are fascinating ideas, especially in light of the world's continuing energy crises.

So let's get back to the *Star Wars* world. If the Force were completely supernatural, that is to say totally above nature, why would life and death—a less efficient and less organized process for the conversion of energy into mechanical work—remain in existence? The Force, or those who become part of the Force, either fully or partially, could auto-correct this inefficiency and there would simply be self-sustaining life. That is not the case in our world or in *Star Wars*. Yoda lives in a decaying swamp, spaceships run on expendable fuel, gardens of food do not just automatically grow—they require cultivation, as far as we know. Owen Lars' moisture farm requires work and machines to collect the water vapors, and there is the distinct possibility that not tending to the machines—"if the units on the south range are not repaired by midday"—will lead to bad things—"there'll be hell to pay." Most importantly, death exists. Beings don't go on living forever. Even Master Yoda dies.

Left alone, nature does find a balance, but it is like the warfare of humans; it is brutal, harsh, and the processes of nature are often violent when they kill off plants and animals in the process. The law of nature is survival of the fittest. There is more than a little truth to evolution, right? We evolve because situations, events, and environments require it. None of this seems very harmonious to me. This is not to say that there is no balance whatsoever in nature, just that the "Great Harmony" as Tai Chi is sometimes called is not as great and harmonious as it once was before the Fall, and will be again after God creates the new earth at the end of time. In the world we live in, it is neither the habit of humans nor the manner of nature to be harmonious or balanced. Gardens don't just grow, and many animals don't just get along.

Why the Force cannot be Divine

Because the Force is often thought of as supernatural, and as such related to God, it is not too far fetched to start thinking that the Force also contains a divine element. The devotion that the Jedi have for it is certainly religious, and they speak of the will of the Force as if it is somehow simultaneously personal and yet above them. Yoda, Obi-Wan, and Qui-Gon all attribute omniscience and omnipotence to the Force.

Here is where I cry, "Danger, danger." To say that the Force only exists as an energy in us and through us and in everything and through everything leads us quickly to say the divine energy is us, and the divine energy is a tree. The partial truths that one being made us as well as the rocks and the trees, that we are all made of similar material, and therefore we all share a similar energy becomes exaggerated to a point when we ignore the opposite truth, that we are also individuals independent of the creative power.

Humans—in all their alien forms—are also inherently different from rocks and trees in *Star Wars*. Rocks and trees don't become Jedi Knights, so the paradox persists that although we are made of similar stuff as the world around us, not only does a separation exist between individual creations, but human creations are greater than rocks and trees. However, we are not gods either. As much as we can be part of the quasi-supernatural Force, we cannot know everything immediately. Luke is not in training because he already knows the Jedi way. If the nature of the *Star Wars* universe—and our own—was towards order and harmony, as in we naturally end up that way, all it would take to be whatever we wanted would be to think it, and it would be so. Even Anakin, a supposed *vergence* of the Force, fathered by midiclorians, must receive training.

Final thoughts

Good stories are like a different kind of apologetic. A successful story is true to the characters as it allows them to do what they would do and not what they should do. Within this context, a story teaches us wrong from right. *Star Wars* is a stellar example of this, if you'll pardon the pun. Compare this cinematic series to *The Matrix* trilogy. *The Matrix* series follows its own philosophy to its logical conclusion instead of following the truth of a story. The result is a savior who is nothing more than a reset button.

Despite what very much <u>seems</u> like the relativity of the light side and the dark side being <u>described</u> as part of the same energy, the *Star Wars* universe does, in fact, <u>depict</u> a world full of moral absolutes where there is no sameness to the powers of light and dark.

[39] DAGOBAH 5—THE DOMAIN OF EVIL CAVE.

Scene— Yoda tells Luke to clear his mind of questions as they take a break from training. Luke sees a huge, dead, black tree with a cave at its base where two large, twisted roots create an opening in the soil.

Luke   —   "There's something not right here. I feel cold, death."

Yoda   —   "That place . . . is strong with the dark side of the Force. A domain of evil it is. In you must go."

Luke   —   "What's in there?"

Yoda   —   "Only what you take with you."
                Luke dons his weapons belt.

Yoda   —   "Your weapons . . . you will not need them."
                Luke walks into the dark and spooky cave, and in a very dream-like sequence, he meets Darth Vader. They duel and Luke easily lobs off Vader's head. As the helmeted head rolls on the ground, part of the face mask explodes to reveal Luke's own face inside the helmet.

Episode V: The Empire Strikes Back

More than just a foreshadowing of Luke's paternity, this scene demonstrates to Luke that it is possible for him to be as evil as Darth Vader. Yoda calls the cave a "domain of evil." How do we become aware of our own potentially evil side? How do we come to understand that we can be deceived into living in such a way that the rest of the world suffers for our convenience—even when we think we are one of the good guys?

Part of the answer to the above question is that we must be active in rooting out evil, however it pops up throughout our lives. The other part of the answer is when Yoda says to Luke, "Your weapons, you will not need them," as Luke prepares to enter the cave. The more tools we acquire in this life, the more difficult it is to learn about the evil nature of ourselves. It would be better for Luke not to take his weapons because he relies on them too quickly. "Live by the sword, die by the sword," is not just a warning against making your living by the oppression of others. Instead, it is a statement of fact: The tool that you choose to make your living is also the tool of your undoing. In *Episode VI: Return of the Jedi,* Yoda describes this experience as a failure of Luke's. Yoda wants him to go in, so that is not Luke's failure. However, Luke chooses to take his weapons into the cave even after Yoda warns him. Luke's choosing weapons represents choosing a violent way of defining and defending himself. These tools also define how he chooses to use the Force. In the cave, Luke uses his lightsaber for aggression, not for knowledge and defense, and this is his failure.

[40] DAGOBAH 6—"DO OR DO NOT. THERE IS NO TRY."

Scene— Luke progresses deeper into his training, and just before Yoda makes the statement in our entry title, we observe Luke standing on his hands with Yoda standing atop Luke's up-raised feet giving Luke instructions on how to lift and pile rocks using only the power of the Force—as in telekinetic movement. R2-D2 beeps furiously as Luke's X-wing fighter begins to sink into the swamp. Luke loses his concentration and everything falls down, including Luke and Yoda.

Episode V: The Empire Strikes Back

Before we sinned, did mankind have telekinetic abilities—and could he fly, etc.? We do not regularly observe people doing these sorts of things, so either these are powers that the vast unused portions of our brain has yet to tap into, or our sin keeps us from these abilities, or both. A fourth option is that we are not meant to do that sort of thing, but that would be a real bummer if it turns out to be true. It is preferable to imagine that on the new earth and in our new bodies, we will be able to do these things.

The lessons that come out of this scene, though, are hugely important and encouraging. Luke complains that he will never get the X-wing out of the muck now.

Yoda — ". . . always with you it cannot be done. Hear you nothing that I say?"

Luke responds that moving an X-wing starfighter is very different from moving stones with his mind. Yoda objects fiercely

Yoda — "No, no different. Only different in your mind. You must unlearn what you have learned."

Luke half-heartedly retorts that he will give it a try. Again Yoda objects.

Yoda — "No! Try not. Do or do not. There is no try."

Episode V: The Empire Strikes Back

Yoda teaches Luke that feeling the Force flowing through him and using it to move rocks is just a first step, meant to be a practice step to show Luke the minimum of what is possible. This is practice in thinking positively. If you start to do something with a negative attitude, or even with an attitude of "giving it a try," then you are much less likely to succeed, and much less likely to enjoy what you are doing. Always with Luke, he looks at what cannot be done, that which was impossible. Luke is like all of us in this respect. We live daily lives of what is probable, and do not expect or often even hope for miracles or great things to happen. Maybe we are too used to disappointment; this is a valid concern. Yoda is teaching Luke hope: Look what you can do with the Force working through you. Look how you can be even more deeply involved with the world around you, Yoda seems to say.

What is it that we must unlearn? We must unlearn the *no*. We must unlearn that only the probable will happen. We must unlearn that we are only physical beings. We must remember the faith of our childhood and make it a mature, adult learning.

The idea of committing fully to something, win or lose, succeed or fail, is an idea we are losing in America. Instead, we tend to do something because it will get us more: more money, more position, etc. If we know or even think that some action will not reap as much benefit for us, we don't do it. There is a balance to this, to be sure. If we never pick up a lost cause, or if we never do something that we know will leave us with less money, less prestige, etc., then our hearts do not learn an important lesson, which is to give more than you receive. It is a true thing that we are more blessed when we give than when we receive. This is a particularly hard thing to do in terms of a career. How do you give selflessly in a career?

Here is another place where Jesus' parable about the talents is valid. A master gives three people different amounts of money while he goes away. He tells each person to invest the money on his behalf. The lesson has as much to do with what we are given as with what we do with it. It is the same when Yoda teaches Luke to use the Force. The Force is strong in Luke. He has a great gift. Yoda wants him to learn to be faithful in the little things so that he can be trusted with learning even greater things. In this scene, Yoda starts with the idea that a willingness to do something completely—commitment to something with no thought of success or failure—opens the ceiling of our expectations to greater things than we ever thought possible. Accomplishing a small task or a large task is first a matter of willingness and desire. Using the Force means understanding that all we need is faith the size of a mustard seed, which is really very tiny (Matthew 17:20), to accomplish incredible tasks. Focusing on limits, as the disciples of Christ did in this Biblical example—they did not believe they can drive out a particularly violent demon—misses the point. The disciples asked themselves, "Do we 'have it in us' to do this difficult thing?" Jesus compares their difficulty to moving a mountain. The point is not to move the mountain. The point is to move ourselves. The total willingness and desire of our spirit, our mind, and our body trusting that God's power can do anything is the point. Yoda says, "There is no try" because if we say, "I will try to do this," we often mean that we will not put our whole selves into doing the task. That is when we are not completely depending on faith, much like Luke did as he flew down the trench of the Death Star. If we say, "I will do this, come what may," then we are committed, and in the doing of that task, success or failure does not matter.

Note to ignorance: This does not mean rushing ill advisedly into anything. The more educated we are, the more fit we are physically, and the more supple to God we make our spirits to be, which is all a life-long process, the better equipped we are *to do*.

Yoda's teaching brings out another important concept that is difficult to understand. Having faith, doing instead of trying, is not a matter of percentages. During college, I attended a gathering of a para-church organization. They handed out an informational card to all guests and asked us to fill out our cards at the end of the meeting. The very last question on the card concerned a person's faith in God. It was one of those. "Do you believe in the Lord as your savior?" or "If you were to die tonight, how sure are you that you would be in heaven?" kind of questions. Interestingly, the answer was multiple choice! One hundred percent, fifty percent, etc. were the options given. The answer to any faith question is always one hundred percent and zero percent, and everything in between, all at the same time. It must be. Calling faith any percent is not only dishonest, for how can we truly measure this, but placing a percentage on the level of our faith is an incorrect statement. It is trying in the way Yoda uses the word. Faith is belief, all the way. Sometimes we feel strong in our faith, and sometimes we wonder if God even exists. The point is not to feel one hundred percent all the time—that is plain dishonesty. Not being honest with yourself in this regard can really stunt God's direction and teaching in your life. Faith cannot be understood scientifically. I scribbled all this down in the margins of the card and received a call from one of the leaders later in the week about my response. The purpose of the call was apparently to check me off like a box: "He is a Christian" or "He is not a Christian," whatever that might mean. I guess he was trying to determine, "Is he going to hell or not? If not, move on." I guess he checked me off as something pretty immediately because he made the conversation very short after my explanation. I do understand his desire to be most effective wherever possible and to "win the lost" in the best way possible. The whole idea of maximizing efficiency, though, is operating out of the idea of percents. I think this is a very prevalent idea today. Trying to tell people about Jesus has become a business plan where we try to reach as many of the lost as possible. Doing church has become more about the machine, the cost effective efficiency of it rather than about caring for the needs of your neighbor. It feels as if we are not showing faith that God will do the canvas calls, the salvation cards, the right marketing to get *them* in the door. I'm all for a logical approach to evangelism, but the craziness we see today does not make me want to be part of the church. This numbers-based approach to evangelism and faith by percentages cuts out the mystical, unquantifiable nature of God, and of his leading.

Learning to do or not is a hard lesson to learn. Luke does not learn it on the first go-round. He starts to lift the X-wing fighter out of the swamp, then thinks about its size. He imagines that bigger means harder. In my research for this book, I looked at internet blogs that discussed *Star Wars* and I came across an entry in World Mag Blog by a woman identified only as "a.b.," whom I was unable to contact.

I want to give her eight-year-old daughter credit for the following image that is an excellent connection between Luke trying to raise the ship and faith.

"a.b." said that her daughter thought the raising of Luke's X-wing from the swamp is very similar to the apostle Peter wanting to walk on the water with Jesus. The disciples are in a boat and they see Jesus walking toward them across the Sea of Galilee. Peter is the picture of active faith when he jumps out of the boat to meet Jesus; he actually walks on the water. Then he sees what he is doing, and even though he is actually walking on the water he knows this is impossible, and starts to sink beneath the surface. Jesus picks him up and together they climb into the boat. Besides the obvious connection of Peter and the X-wing sinking in the water, both the apostle Peter and Luke Skywalker allow a supernatural power to work in and through them to levitate mass and defy gravity. More importantly, both have a failure of faith, directly after experiencing amazing successes. Thanks "a.b." and daughter. That is great imagery!

[41] DAGOBAH 7—"MY ALLY IS THE FORCE."

Scene— Luke fails to raise the X-wing fighter out of the muck, exclaiming in exhaustion that the starfighter spacecraft is too big to move. Yoda chastises Luke, asking him if he judges Yoda by his size. Size does not matter when we let go of our ego and allow faith to work. Luke shakes his head to indicate that he does not judge Yoda by his size.

Yoda　　－　"And well you should not. For my ally is the Force. And a powerful ally it is. Life creates it, makes it grow. Its energy surrounds us and binds us. Luminous beings are we . . . (Yoda pinches Luke's shoulder) . . . not this crude matter. You must feel the Force around you. Here, between you . . . me . . . the tree . . . the rock . . . everywhere! Yes, even between land and ship."

Luke　　－　"You want the impossible."

Episode V: The Empire Strikes Back

These are my favorite words in all the *Star Wars* movies. I do so want to believe in this Force. God created a world full of energy, full of growing life, and there is a commonality of us all with nature. Our bodies are natural, part of the universe, and separating ourselves from the ground completely is not good for us. We are carbon-based life forms, after all. Can't you feel the power of nature when you are in it? Magnify that feeling more and more and you get what it will be like to be in the world God has made without our sin.

The Force all around us is also roughly similar to slowing your mind through concentration and meditation, which leads to the realization that we can connect to God. We can tap into his creative energy, which is in everything, including ourselves, because he made us. This is called General Revelation.

When we unabashedly put ourselves into the right thing at the right time God blesses that work and we can feel God's Spirit flowing in, through, and around us. In other words, the Force being with us is like in baseball when you swing the bat as best as you can at your pitch. The result of the smooth, complete movement is the bat connecting with the ball as you smash it out of the ballpark. It may even seem that God is conspiring to help us succeed. Keep in mind that this metaphor is true for whatever work God has for you. It could mean dying for his sake. Even if it doesn't involve actual death, then it may seem very similar. We do know that we are to "take up our cross daily." By this, Jesus means we must take up the work that he intends for us, primarily loving our neighbors as ourselves, and secondarily whatever we are drawn to as an occupation. This is not at all a health and wealth gospel.

Feeling the energy of the Force is also like music. For me rock music especially communicates this feeling. The band playing on a stage creates a moment that transcends the moment itself. There is almost something holy about a great song played by a great band in a great venue. These moments of transcendence can also happen with recorded music, especially when driving in a car. These moments contain the essence of myth stories. Joseph Campbell, who taught and wrote about myth for many years, and who heavily influenced George Lucas once said that we need myths,

> "so that our life experiences on the purely physical plane will have resonances within our own innermost being and reality, so that we actually feel the rapture of being alive."[9]
> (*The Power of Myth*, Campbell/Moyers, p. 5)

Continuing the above quote, Bill Moyers asked Joseph Campbell, "How do you get that experience?" Campbell responded, "Read myths." He made a point of saying that it is good to read the myths of traditions other than your own because the realness of your own traditions can prohibit your mind from getting in touch with the experience of being alive. Myth is even more than that, though. Wanting to feel the Force around us, letting great music transport us, escaping to another world in a book or movie are all examples of the reality of God and our desire to experience him and chase after him in as many different ways as we can. Not only is it a valid practice for someone who worships Christ to find him in locations other than strictly Christian places, but it is extremely important for us to do this. If you are a Christian, you may be thinking, "You're right, Caleb. This is a great opportunity to show Christ to others. What an evangelism tool!" Don't go there. That is missing my point. Myth is important to you, reader, as an individual. This is God's gift to you. We all are chasing him in some way, and when we find an experience that helps us know we are alive, as *Star Wars* does for me and likely you, too, you love the myth first. Joseph Campbell, and likely George Lucas, might disagree with me that myth echoes truth, truth does not echo myth. The difference is a belief that God exists. Truth exists outside of us so that we can discover it as opposed to god—small "g"—existing merely inside of us. This forces our concept of truth into whatever it is at the moment we think we are discovering within ourselves. When you love the myth of *Star Wars*, you are enjoying God in that place. For me, the mythic parts of *Star Wars* echo the truth that someday I will glorify God on a higher plane, to a greater reality than I am now able.

I once attended a Leanne Payne conference. One of the first things she asked us was whether we knew that our spirits are larger than our bodies. We have a spirit that we must also learn about and nurture. This is like Yoda saying, "Luminous beings are we . . . not this crude matter." Yoda was not saying that Luke was not also a physical being—crude matter—but he was helping Luke understand that we are not just and only a physical body. As a side-note, in my opinion, this is the greatest reason why we need to exercise much more care with abortion. It is not just crude matter we are dealing with in the mother and the baby and the father. All three are luminous beings, and we need to think of ourselves and others in that way.

Leanne Payne also has much to say about practicing Christ's presence in our lives. This is the only accurate way to use the Force and to feel the Force around us in our real lives. The Force in the *Star Wars* movies loses much in this translation. Much is left out that, in real life, is at once harder, more defined, and more rewarding than the generic Force of the movies. Practicing the presence of the living God involves worship, prayer, study, dedication of your life and your life's work to God, and allowing the Holy Spirit to bring out love, joy, peace, patience, kindness, gentleness, goodness, faithfulness, and self control in your life. These things will help you feel, channel, use, and become powerful in the part of the Force that really does exist. If you love the *Star Wars* movies, and love the idea of the Force, you are probably like me in that you keep seeing Luke on that mound looking into the double sunset. You hear the music, and you experience a longing—an aching—that makes your spirit want to emanate out of you and say, "Yes, that's it. I am longing for it. I am even longing to be on the journey to it."

This is the longing of the separation of our souls from God. We are longing to be home and in his presence.

Scene: Yoda concentrates, then, using the power of the Force, Yoda raises Luke's now submerged X-wing starfighter completely out of the swamp and onto dry ground.

Luke   –   "I . . . I don't believe it."
Yoda   –   "This is why you fail."

                              Episode V: The Empire Strikes Back

The interesting thing here is that failing or succeeding is not just a matter of our abilities. Our belief of whether we can do a thing also is a factor. It is possible, therefore, to possess the ability to do something, but if we do not believe we can do that task, we may never realize our potential, or use those talents that we already possess.

[42] THE GROWTH OF HAN SOLO, LEIA ORGANA, AND LANDO CALRISSIAN.

These three characters, in classic Act II form, are in the middle of their growth as well.

Han Solo is learning to be responsible, and vulnerable. He is in charge of many people. He is a commander. Instead of being the last person to volunteer, he is the only one who leaves the shelter of the Rebel Alliance base on Hoth and risks his life to find his friend, Luke Skywalker. From what we know of Han's life before this scene, we gather that he has no affection for the Empire, and in *Episode V: The Empire Strikes Back*, he exhibits actual disdain for the Empire. He acts tirelessly in escaping from the Empire's minions, and Han's efforts eventually cost the Empire a great many lost ships and dead pilots. Given all this, and all his involvement in the resistance, Han also understands that eventually he must face Jabba, and pay him off soon.

Another sign of Han's growing maturity is evident when he faces Darth Vader in Cloud City. Han has no hesitation and immediately responds with pure reflex in drawing his blaster. Even a smuggler from low places recognizes evil as evil. Han Solo also expresses, although still a bit stilted, his affection for Leia. A big test for Han occurs when he is a guinea pig for the trap Vader sets for Luke on Cloud City. Vader tortures Han for no apparent reason, and is eventually frozen in a block of carbonite. Han's final response is not anger toward his aggressors, but rather an instruction for Chewbacca to take care of Princess Leia. In this trial, Han overcame his selfishness. He shows that he is willing to die for his friends.

We get the feeling that Leia has been a leader since she was very young. Her biggest issue, far and away, is that her bossiness prevents her from discovering more of the Force, receiving the power by letting go. She has a hard time letting go of anything, and it stifles her relationship with Han. Forced to escape Hoth with Han, she faces the test of simply being with Han, feeling his affection towards her, and having to react. She then must force herself to trust his wild plans for plunging into a deadly asteroid field and hiding in a crater, then trusting his old gambling buddy with repairs to the *Millennium Falcon*. Leia is a logical, no-nonsense woman, and these shenanigans of Han's must be very difficult for her.

We get our first glimpse of Lando Calrissian mid-way through this film. We are quickly caught up with his life through his conversation with Han. He is a gambler who won Cloud City in a game of chance. Instead of squandering it or gambling it away, he seemingly becomes the competent administrator/governor of it. He, like Han, is learning responsibility that rubs against the cowboy image that he so desires. Lando does not have much of a choice when the Empire arrives, and though we usually think of him at first as a bad guy for not slipping the news to Han and Leia and allowing them to escape and warn Luke, the decision is more difficult than we want to admit. Lando has many people under him to look after, as well as the inhabitants of Cloud City. Darth Vader shows up unexpectedly with an entire fleet of Star Destroyers and an ultimatum for Lando to help him or everyone dies. Lando perhaps could be more creative than just giving in, but Darth Vader is not breathing down *our* necks, so let's not be too quick to judge. Lando and Han have some of the same lessons to learn: Each must make hard decisions that involve many people and give of himself. Lando essentially leaves his wealth and power behind in an attempt to catch Boba Fett with Leia and Chewy. At the end of the film, Lando decides to pursue Han's release, and this decision does not seem to be at all contrived. Lando earnestly undertakes this mission with both heart and soul. Finally, we see him commanding part of the fleet in *Episode VI: Return of the Jedi*, so we know that Lando does grow to be a better person through the trials of these films.

It is interesting to note that all three of these characters have a tendency to hold on tightly to what they want for themselves. The element of growth that we see in them all, the practice that allows them to perform better in their missions, is to help others and become greater by letting go of their individual egos and the interpretation of success their egos had previously built for them.

[43] A weeping and gnashing of teeth.

In *Episode V: The Empire Strikes Back*, the Empire demonstrates the growth of evil characters in a directly opposite fashion from the growth of Han Solo, Luke Skywalker, Princess Leia Organa, and Lando Calrissian.

Darth Vader says, "Apology accepted, Captain Needa," after he tele-kinetically chokes Captain Needa to death for making one mistake too many. Vader gives Needa no grace, no mentoring that we can see, and no positive reinforcement of any kind. In fact, it is unlikely that the Empire uses any kind of positive anything in the training of its soldiers and officers. This is the Empire's way. "No time" could be its mantra. The dark side is always tearing people down. Backbiting, lying, cheating, and self promotion are common tactics, no doubt, in the struggle for promotion. This is what I imagine the gnashing of teeth in hell must be like.

In the kind of world the Empire creates through total domination and fear, even those who serve the Emperor and Vader fear for their lives. Does Vader make it clear how he wants things done? This is doubtful. Instead, he judges those whose performance he does not approve, and kills them if they do something he really dislikes. The qualities of just how "star systems will slip through [their] fingers," as Leia states in *Episode IV: A New Hope*, comes through as we watch the bad guys function. With such strict, cold, unforgiving, over-organization, the Empire became powerful, but it is not at all difficult to imagine the Empire's implosion. Who wants to remain in that kind of society?

Sometimes elements of the Empire symbolize America's current over-emphasis on work, control, and bottom-lining everything. Everything must have a business plan and make a profit. This pernicious practice of making everything a functioning business results in our obsession with more. For so many media companies, the occupation is no longer journalism—reporting on what is happening in the world, both good and bad, political or non—it is about selling information to the masses. When we see news shows that are extremely shiny productions, does anyone actually believe what the announcers say? Too often, we do buy into that slick packaging. Better would be to take a step back from the show and ask, "What is it they want me to think?" Those news shows will hardly seem credible once you do this, and once you seek the truth of a piece of news that the show presents.

The same thing is happening in our churches, art galleries, halls of government, and even within many businesses. The reality of God, the truth of art, the serving of others, or the selling of a thing to a person who actually needs that item tends to be replaced with the mentality of doing it simply for the money or to make a person feel good. It is true that marketing works, that business plans work, that efficiency models work, that tax lawyers work. However, many of us are getting tired of this Empire-ical emphasis. We would like to do something simply for the love of giving ourselves to that thing, and for the sake of doing it. Just because we can be more efficient in most ways of life does not mean it is a good thing to do everything more efficiently. We are missing the learning part of the process, we are missing ourselves—and other people—in the process. We are missing the love and the devotion. In short, it sometimes feels as if we live in the Empire, or in the Republic just before it becomes the Empire.

[44] WHAT WE DO NOT KNOW.

Luke Skywalker realizes early on that there is much of the Force that he does not understand. Part of this is due to the environment of learning on the run and training informally. This fosters an idea within Luke that there is much for him to learn, so he looks for training anywhere he can.

The first three movies, also known as the prequels, present a completely different world, where the Jedi are extremely dominant and prolific. There is a Jedi academy and a huge organization that supports it, including the incredible Jedi library seen in *Episode II: Attack of the Clones*. In the midst of this wealth of power, the Jedi Council becomes comfortable, maybe even proud, and this leads to its decline. Members of the Jedi Council do not have Luke's sense of wonder. The Jedi of this world are trained from the age of toddlers. This may cause the complacency that prevents them from relating individually to the Force. Similarly, we can become so involved with church that we forget how to speak outside of that dialect, and then we forget to understand the individuality of the Messiah's connection with each of us in a unique and personal, magical way. We see this when a preacher fails to admit that he does not know something. None of us knows all things, and it is a sign of wisdom to admit when we don't. This happens in the academic and scientific worlds as well. In the church and in the university these days, there is such a consciousness of how much mankind knows. In contrast, Luke understands the importance of acknowledging that he does not know everything. His perspective is that there is much of life and much of the Force yet to discover.

Where is the admission in our world of those things that are not known? For example, it is a commonly held opinion that we evolved from apes. Semantics—the way a concept is stated—is vitally important. We stagnate ourselves when we say, "We evolved from apes" because this is a statement of permanent knowledge, even though this statement actually represents only our best guess at this time. The statement is, of course, partly untrue. We do not actually know we came from apes, or for that matter that the whole of mankind originated from a shrew living in the age of dinosaurs before we became apes. Many scientists believe, based on all the information now available to them, that this is the case. The issue I have with this theory is that it is stated as truth. Stating that we know we came from apes might make as much a fool of scientists as the church leaders of Galileo's day. Galileo's work told him the Earth was not flat. The church would not hear of it. A hundred years from now science may think man must be a unique creation and could never have originated from the apes. Ironically enough, it is the discipline of always understanding we do not know everything that allows us to discover, learn, then *know* more.

Like the church in Galileo's day, and like Anakin, we can end up on the dark side even though we intend to represent the light side. We can become agents of evil, and it might start with a statement as innocuous as saying "we came from apes" instead of the more precise "we think we came from apes." It seems like such a harmless mistake, but here is where this sort of thinking has already lead: It was commonplace in the college from which I graduated for professors to comment that a belief in God was ridiculous because of evolution. How we get to promoting an idea that there is no God from the theories of evolution is like saying Homer never existed because we lack his DNA sample, therefore, someone else must have written his stories. The two are completely different disciplines! If a student had questions at this institution of higher learning and tried to reconcile his or her religious views with the professor's own evolutionistic or feministic beliefs, the professor would often ridicule that student publicly in the classroom. This created an environment where questioning along these lines, or any lines that might disagree with a professor, proved detrimental to any student. The university environment is supposed to be a place where we learn how to think, how to question, and how to disagree. Instead, it seems—from my experience and from reading the experiences of others—that universities are becoming more and more homogenous. This reminds me of Anakin wanting to make everyone agree, and how the seed of this urge turns Anakin into Darth Vader, who strikes terror into anyone who might dare disagree with him.

[45] LUKE SEES THE FUTURE . . . MAYBE.

Scene: Luke stands on his hands doing Jedi exercises while his mind, using the power of the Force, lifts boxes and R2-D2 into the air. Yoda instructs him about how he might see visions of the future. Then, in Luke's mind he sees Han Solo and Princess Leia in the Cloud City, and they seem to be in pain. Luke asks Yoda whether they will die.

Yoda   —   "Difficult to see. Always in motion the future is."
                   Luke says that he must go to them.

Yoda   —   "Decide you must how to serve them best. If you leave now, help them you could. But you would destroy all for which they have fought and suffered."

Episode V: The Empire Strikes Back

Seeing the future is not part of our common experience. And future-telling is not something God wants us to do; not only because this practice belongs to the dark side, but also because it takes our minds off what is most important, which is knowing him and worshipping him in the here and now, having faith in a future we can't see.

This dialogue contains something very special. Rushing into something unprepared or unfocused, as Luke does, can actually cause our mission to fail.

Yoda helps Luke decide; he does not try to coerce him. Instead, he pleads the case of wisdom. The Force, like love, cannot be pushed on people. When you try to push love on people, it does not work. Love is not the result of this coercive effort. Love resists overpowering control. Even in Yoda's desperation to save Luke, Yoda understands that forcing Luke to remain means using the very dark side from which he seeks to protect Luke.

Yoda   —   "Luke! You must complete the training."

Luke   —   "I can't keep the vision out of my head. They're my friends. I've got to help them."

Yoda   —   "You must not go!"

Luke   —   "But Han and Leia will die if I don't."

Now Ben Kenobi's Force ghost chimes in:

Ben   –   "You don't know that. Even Yoda cannot see their fate."

Luke   –   "But I can help them! I feel the Force!"

Ben   –   "But you cannot control it. This is a dangerous time for you, when you will be tempted by the dark side of the Force."

Episode V: The Empire Strikes Back

Everyone is tested in their faith. The parable of the seeds is a good analogy to the concerns expressed by Ben and Yoda. They know that someone young in the faith can be tested and fail, and failure is especially likely if that person has not completed training. This would be like a seed falling on shallow ground. It grows for a little but does not have enough soil, enough foundation, to continue to grow.

Luke is also like a recent enlistee into the military. No officer sends a new recruit, especially one who has yet to complete basic training, into battle against an elite U.S. Army Ranger or a U.S. Navy Seal.

Yoda   –   "Yes, yes. To Obi-Wan you listen. The cave. Remember your failure at the cave!"

Luke   –   "But I've learned so much since then. Master Yoda, I promise to return and finish what I've begun. You have my word."

Yoda refers here to Luke's walk into the cave on Dagobah and use of the dark side of the Force in anger, prompted by his dependence upon weapons. Yoda knows that Luke's temptation to turn to the dark side is not only possible, but likely. Especially if Luke uses brute strength and technology, such as his weapons in the cave, in any situation where he lacks full understanding. In fact, this is the Emperor's expectation and plan.

Ben   –   "It is you and your abilities the Emperor wants. That is why your friends are made to suffer."

Luke   –   "That is why I have to go."

Ben	—	"Luke, I don't want to lose you to the Emperor the way I lost Vader."
Luke	—	"You won't."
Yoda	—	"Stopped they must be. On this all depends. Only a fully trained Jedi Knight with the Force as his ally will conquer Vader and his Emperor. If you end your training now, if you choose the quick and easy path, as Vader did, you will become an agent of evil."
Ben	—	"Patience."
Luke	—	"And sacrifice Han and Leia?"
Yoda	—	"If you honor what they fight for . . . yes!"

Episode V: The Empire Strikes Back

Ben and Yoda also understood that a little knowledge is a dangerous thing. This stage in Luke's development is similar to that of a young Christian who is sometimes not able to tell good teaching from bad, orthodoxy from cult. A young Christian may not be able to understand deeper theology or the reality of the Holy Spirit. These are difficult concepts even for mature Christians. A young Christian is susceptible to emotional appeals or wild encouragement, exaggerated theologies, and practices that end up creating disillusionment until they learn to see through these tactics. For example, Luke's sensing things through the Force is like our learning about the spirit world. We become very excited when we first understand this is a real thing. After all, this settles many issues of whether God exists or not . . . doesn't it? Awareness of the reality of angels and demons must also inform us in this way. Our place in this realm, as in the effects of our worship, prayer, and faith, does not really belong to the tangible, physical world, does it? In the end, we must all have a presence in the spirit world, much as we see in *Star Wars*. A new Christian may experience an emotional downer when he or she realizes Christians are not to practice divination, sorcery, or witchcraft, or even to try to command, bind, or toss out demons without asking Jesus. Failure to rely only and exclusively on Jesus, the source of a Christian's light side, can only bring evil and pain into our lives. Often, we realize that use of the Force is not as direct, not as known, and not as magical as we see in the movies or read in books. Many Christians lose their faith at this point. Of course, many Christians may also lose their faith in churches that ignore the spiritual nature of whom God has created us to be.

Under such disillusionment, Luke would not likely have lost his faith in the Force, but rather become enchanted by the easy power of the Force, and wonder why Ben and Yoda always seemed to want him to do things the hard way. This is same way the dark side attracts us in real life, too. Luke does not live in the spirit world of the Force, but learns to use it in the real world. This is like our existence on earth. We are in the physical world. We are not meant to be all spirit. Take, for example, the power of witchcraft, even when the person practicing it intends its use for only good. To use witchcraft and sorcery, etc., is wrong because we are not able to see behind this part of the Force to understand its evil. For a deeper explanation of this topic, read Catherine Edwards Sanders' book, *The Charm of Wicca.* Yoda and Ben see much of Anakin in Luke, and they are gravely concerned that if Luke is seduced into thinking there is validity in the dark side, then the son might repeat the story of the father when the Emperor used this dualism to deceive Anakin.

Ben	–	"If you choose to face Vader, you will do it alone. I cannot interfere."
Luke	–	"I understand."
Ben	–	"Luke, don't give in to hate. That leads to the dark side."
Yoda	–	"Strong is Vader. Mind what you have learned. Save you it can."
Luke	–	"I will. And I'll return. I promise."

Episode V: The Empire Strikes Back

Luke acts as recklessly as they fear he might. Yoda voices true concerns in his little cave before training Luke. Not giving in to hate is the key when all else fails, especially when we are acting with a hot head, prone to exaggeration, or something rash temps us, even to the point of giving in to the dark side.

[46] DARTH VADER TRAPS LUKE.

Much of the plot of *Episode V: The Empire Strikes Back* deals with Darth Vader's attempts to catch Luke. If Vader senses Luke's presence, why does he not sense Yoda's? Is Yoda so accomplished that he is able to hide his presence? Why Obi Wan and Yoda do not at least consider changing Luke's last name when he is born and place him with a family not related to Vader's, as they do with Princess Leia, is quite beyond my capacity. At any rate, Vader is out to catch Luke not simply because Luke is his son, but much like when Satan tries to catch Job, he too was strong in the Force, and a faithful soul.

Vader finally has his opportunity to set a trap for Luke on Cloud City. Although Luke's progress in the Jedi training impresses Vader during times of battle, Vader does not even need to use both hands to fight Luke until the end of their duel, and only then because he tires of Luke's persistence and pushes him out onto a ledge in the center of the guts of Cloud City, and slices off Luke's right hand.

"Luke, it is your destiny," Vader says to try and persuade Luke to join the dark side. He even offers him a share of the Empire. "Together we can rule the universe as father and son," and "the Emperor has foreseen it," Vader offers. How much is this like Satan tempting Jesus? Vader, and Satan, each offer control of the world to those they tempt. The drama of the moment notwithstanding, realizing that your father is not dead, but instead is a powerful and influential man who wants you as his right hand man, is a very alluring proposition. Satan's use of a morsel of truth to deceive us is extremely common, however. The morsel offered here is that Luke is Vader's son. The rest of the truth is that Vader is hardly Anakin any longer. He is a different being: physically he is more robot than human, and spiritually he is Sith.

Many of us are misled into bad places through similar half-truths. How many religions or cults use half-truths to entice members? How many of us respond foolishly when televangelists con us out of money? As a people, we are very much like sheep. We often fall for things that look good only on the surface. We fail to question further.

Another half-truth from Vader is his temptation of Luke with a presumed destiny. It is true that it is Luke's destiny to become powerful in the Force, however he is able to use either the light side or the dark side to become so. At least Ben and Yoda warn him not to be tempted by the easy power of the dark side. Vader wants to control Luke into joining the dark side, and this is what stands out to Luke and prevents him from choosing that path. It is a universal truth that when someone uses control tactics and fear to get you to do something, it would be a good and healthy thing for us to back away. Luke's great love for his friends also keeps him from moving to the dark side. How many times do friends and family stop us from doing something bad? And how many times does your love for them help you resist doing something that otherwise you might well do? Good and wise friends help us make good and wise decisions, and their presence in our lives keeps us from the dark side.

[47] Luke lets go.

When Darth Vader hovers over Luke, coaxing him to join the dark side, Luke lets go of his precarious hold on the spire and falls down the main shaft. He essentially gives up his life. In this moment, he demonstrates a greater maturity than ever before. It might mean his death, and if it had, Luke would have had an honorable end, a heroic end, and it still makes a great story. This scene is like James 4, which is all about selfish desires and split loyalties, and this is at the core of Luke's temptation to join Vader. Verse 7 of the fourth chapter of James says, "Resist the devil, and he will flee from you. Come near to God and he will come near to you . . . ." Vader is hardly fleeing from Luke. However, when Luke says, "I'll never join you," and falls down the shaft, he is resisting the devil. The fall is a good metaphor for a "leap of faith," which is to come near to God.

He falls down and is mercifully saved by an exhaust tube, which drops him out of the bottom of the floating cloud city. There, Luke dangles on an antenna, crying out for Ben or Leia to save him. Through this amazing sequence of trials, Luke does not dwell on the surprise of his survival. His concentration is on the here and now. Where he is and what he does saves Luke, and his rescue is inspiring. Through all of his adventure, Luke doesn't focus on his failure, he keeps his head.

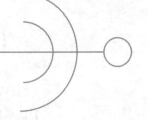

EPISODE VI
RETURN OF THE JEDI

[48] MORE FEAR TACTICS, FROM THE TOP DOWN.
VADER SPEAKS TO COMMANDER MOFF JERJERROD
IN THE NEW DEATH STAR AT THE BEGINNING
OF *EPISODE VI: RETURN OF THE JEDI*.

Darth Vader arrives at the new, half-constructed Death Star II. Apparently, Commander Moff Jerjerrod is behind schedule in its completion, yet he contends that his men are working as fast as they can. Regardless of what is the truth, Vader starts straight off with threats. "Perhaps I can find new ways to motivate them," he tells Jerjerrod. *Them* refers to the workers, and fear tactics are implied. The commander admits that, in his opinion, the Emperor is asking the impossible. Jerjerrod needs more men. Vader tells him that the Emperor will soon arrive, and that for the commander's own sake, he hopes the job will be completed when the Emperor wants it, and without any more men than originally allotted because, "the Emperor is not as forgiving as I am," Vader warns darkly.

The reason why myths like *Star Wars* are so good for us is that they tend to put good and bad into a very clear light. In the everyday world, the lines are a bit more cloudy. We all have a little good and a little bad in us, and it is easy to sometimes get confused with right and wrong to the point we don't even think they exist. Myth stories bring us back, show us clearly the good and the bad, and help us to realign our perspectives.

[49] C-3PO and R2-D2 at
Jabba the Hutt's Palace:
How do you know when you are
in a bad place . . . isn't it obvious?

C-3PO and R2-D2 walk up to Jabba's rusty, steel-domed palace. The droids thus introduce us to Jabba's dark den of mafia-like power and low-life epicurean delights. This place is reckless, wild, and lawless, except for what suits Jabba's pleasure. C-3PO absolutely abhors the place even before he walks inside. It is not a subtly bad place. Jabba personifies the world he creates; the slug-like creature's body is one large piece of fat, and he seems to be as comfortable with chaos as he is with controlling others. Even with Luke and company's escape when pandemonium breaks out on Jabba's sail barge, Jabba seems to revel in this end and is quite entertained up until the point when Leia strangles him with her chain leash. Jabba is the end result of belief in a material world and the enjoyment of the body. Jabba's Palace is more like a lair, seedy through and through.

In the same way Darth Vader's character is revealed in the environment of the elite and sophisticated Star Destroyer, or Yoda in the simple nature of Dagobah, Jabba and his desert palace epitomize an exaggerated character in an exaggerated condition—a mythic condition—that we know a little bit about from our own world. Often, though, we do not recognize bad people in their bad places until we relate them to the characters we read about in stories. No doubt, Jabba's palace is a bad place. However, do we always know when we are in a bad place, either physically or spiritually?

There are those reading this book who might enjoy and identify with our equivalent of Jabba's palace, which might include strip clubs, sex shops, violent gang hang-outs, drug parlors, and seedy bars, etc. No one goes to those places rightly thinking they are havens of goodness, safety, and unconditional love. Not that every place you could go should be Aunt Bea's kitchen, but what about those places that you might more easily be convinced are OK? Many places in our culture use women's bodies to sell things. Soft porn is pervasive on TV, the internet, and in the movies. Romance novels—many of them the equivalent of porn for women—are a booming part of the publishing business. Violence—whether in news, cartoons, or drama serials—is seen as a must to attract viewers. America is often a place where men and women gain respect from money, and society isn't very particular about how they obtain it. We live in a funnel. The broad part on top is our general, everyday world, where many of the things accentuated in Jabba's Palace are not taken to extremes. In fact, most of these seem really rather harmless, such as a commercial for underwear that uses an impossibly gorgeous model. The narrow or bottom part is the world I mention in the beginning of the paragraph. Many of the harmless things at the top of the funnel slip down into the classic deadly vices at the bottom of our funnel.

How does *Star Wars* deal with these degradations? For one, the movies portray them for what they are. Second, they treat these moral degradations in a very Old Testament fashion. In the Old Testament, God often purges evil or directs his people to do so. Look at the Old Testament stories of the judges and prophets. Their message was, "Repent from your evil ways, turn to the one true God and be saved." Either the people do repent and gain salvation, or they don't, and many are killed. There was one judge named Ehud, who was left-handed. When the Israelites finally repented, Ehud was sent to assassinate King Eglon, a Moabite, who had conquered Israel eighteen years earlier as a result of Israel's idol worship. Ehud strapped a double-edged, foot-and-a-half-long knife to his right thigh, got the King alone and plunged it into the King's belly. The King was so fat, and Ehud drove the blade in so deep, that the King's stomach swallowed up even the handle of Ehud's weapon. It is not too far-fetched to imagine that Luke might just as easily have plunged a lightsaber into Jabba's many layers of fat. Now, Luke did not set his friends in place to bring about repentance in Jabba the Hutt, or to free a people who had repented. Luke and Lando are there solely to free Han, who in his carbonite state does seem to be in perpetual anguish. As a result, Han does come away from the experience a much wiser person. Meanwhile, the situation itself—the raw violence that is the destruction of Jabba and all his cohorts on the party barge in the desert—with enemies falling into the pit of the great Sarlacc, are definitely Old Testament images that are so politically incorrect.

The sequence at Jabba's Palace brings out one other thing worthy of mention. Men who ogle women—and most men at least have this temptation—must see a little of themselves in Jabba as he takes pleasure in the dancing of a green girl, then in watching Leia in her metal bikini. If you see your actions or behavior resembling Jabba's to any extent, you cannot be happy with yourself. Sometimes it takes seeing an exaggerated character in its own environment to recognize the temptation of sin that exists in all of us.

[50] And God saw that it was good. Evangelism in the post-Christian world.

We all tend to gravitate toward stories that share our view of the world. Although many people who believe in Jesus enjoy *Star Wars* a great deal, the concept that the Force has a light side and a dark side and the relationship between the Force and a supernatural being turns other Christians off to enjoying the parts of *Star Wars* to which they do agree. What they miss is a great depth of enjoyment and solid teaching to their children on how to see and deal with the good and the bad in our world. Sure, there is an occasional Bible study or teaching series that references *Star Wars*, but it seems that this is mostly done because church parishioners watch *Star Wars* and the clergy use these movies as a frame of reference for some other topic. Perhaps *Star Wars* is used as a springboard for discussion. In their proper settings, these uses are fine and good. The danger here is that it can seem a little contrived, as if mentioning *Star Wars* suddenly makes another topic more interesting and less boring. In addition, and this is really sad, *Star Wars* may be mentioned without any love for the movies themselves.

A big concern for Christians is that we do not become part of the world in the sense that we love other things more than we love God. This is a very valid concern. There is also the opposite concern, which is that we must engage the world around us. More than just simply existing in a subculture, the lack of personally expressing and explaining "Yes!" to the good and "No!" to the bad—as opposed to the canned corporate religious response can really affect the world in which we live.

We must face what many of us fear: we must seek to enjoy something that is not explicitly about God or something that does not explicitly talk about religious subjects. At the same time, we must not enjoy something without filtering it through our religious beliefs. God did not create the whole universe and say, "This is good because it reminds me of myself," although there is much truth in this statement. It is important that God called his creation good. He enjoyed, and continues to enjoy, his creation. The fact that a creation of his exists is good on its own. The fact that a creation of ours exists is good on its own in so far as we have made it for good. We are, however, obviously much more prone to create something bad or mediocre than good or great.

Here is the stickler: we now must show love in this way in order to evangelize. The post-Christian world is similar to the world of Jesus and Paul. Jesus was a Jew, but he had to communicate a larger truth to Jews, who often did not see the spirit behind the law, and were not ready for the Messiah. Still, Jesus met them in their own Judaism. The apostle Paul did the same when he spoke with the Greeks and Romans. He was a citizen of Rome, a Jew, and also a Christian. He met his audiences face-to-face and in their own cultures. To the Greeks, Paul introduced the unknown God; to the Romans, righteousness. In a like manner, Christians today must show Jesus to those who have no concept of him other than cultural points of common reference. This begins with love; love for your place, love for your time, love for the culture around you. More than the words that might come from us such as, "Jesus is like . . ." this love requires us first to simply be. We are to exist in this world. Next, we are to take part in calling something good when it is good.

[51] LUKE ARRIVES AT JABBA'S PALACE. MORE JEDI TRICKS THAT SKYWALKER HAS LEARNED.

When Luke arrives at Jabba's Palace, he uses some form of Jedi power on the pig-like guards. He points a finger at them and they back away from him, reeling. Then he uses the Jedi mind trick on Bib Fortuna, whom Luke commands to arrange an immediate audience with Jabba. In front of Jabba, however, Luke does not fare as well. Still, he maintains his cool and his confidence.

The whole beginning of *Episode VI: Return of the Jedi* demonstrates Luke's growth as a Jedi. He practices, and most likely sits quietly for long periods, meditating on what he has learned. Luke has a presence about him. This is a presence of authority, of knowledge, of conviction. Preachers often appear this way, as do some professors. Any person who has a difficult job that requires much learning and studying well understands Luke's frame of mind.

Two music leaders serve a church I previously attended. One could hardly be described as anything but anointed in his task. When he played and led worship, the Holy Spirit was very often present in a tangible way. This was not hokey or contrived. He had real authority in his work that stemmed, first, from his competence as a musician, and second, from possessing the gift of the Holy Spirit in his work. The second leader was talented enough musically, but it was as if he was striving too hard to force the Holy Spirit's presence. There were things he would say and do that sounded spiritually grandiose. It almost seemed as if he was trying to jump-start the high of the Holy Spirit's presence. His methods did not work. There would be an early swell of participation by the audience that quickly went flat.

In *Episode VI: Return of the Jedi*, Luke is well on his way to possessing mastery of the Force. Some of his confidence seems faked, though. It does not seem as if he is prepared to meet the rancor, for example, and why did he use the Force to grab one of the guard's blasters before he fell down the chute? He did not seem to be using the Force in those moments. He does engineer their escape, however planned it was or wasn't, and he proves that he has authority in the Jedi arts. And so it is with us. We are tested, and that testing is good and necessary. If we think we know something, if we think we have authority in a certain discipline or area of life, testing will bring it out. The air of authority can be faked, however. There are plenty of people who convince us that they can do, know, or be a certain thing. Appearances can be, and often are, deceiving. Only performance will bring out the true worth of these individuals.

[52] THE EMPEROR ARRIVES AT DEATH STAR II.
HOW TO KNOW WHEN THE LEADER OF YOUR
RELIGION OR GOVERNMENT HAS GONE TOO FAR.

The Emperor arrives at the new Death Star. There is a full military formation awaiting him, his Red Guards precede him, sickly fortune-telling men in flowing robes follow him, and the next highest ranking person in the government, Darth Vader, kneels before him. This is an extreme picture of a front man with too much power. By the time you have one of these as your leader, it's too late; a revolution is the only thing for it.

The Emperor does not start out like this, however. Not many of them do. It is valuable to see the Emperor's elevation to power in the three movie prequels, where at first the Emperor seems a normal and benevolent old man. Gradually, the movies uncover his sinuous and treacherous evil nature. This is a good warning. The problem is, when you see the Emperor arriving in the way he does in *Episode VI: Return of the Jedi*, you know it is already too late for a regime change. Individual freedoms are already curtailed, dissenting voices silenced, and military might unchecked and controlled by only one person. How many countries on our planet are either already there or well on the way? How can you know when the leader of your religion or government has gone too far, possibly even before he or she has?

In Matthew 7:15–20, Jesus says,

> "Watch out for false prophets. They come to you in sheep's clothing, but inwardly they are ferocious wolves. By their fruit you will recognize them. Do people pick grapes from thorn-bushes, or figs from thistles? Likewise every good tree bears good fruit, but a bad tree bears bad fruit. A good tree cannot bear bad fruit, and a bad tree cannot bear good fruit. Every tree that does not bear good fruit is cut down and thrown into the fire. Thus, by their fruit you will recognize them."

In this context, fruit is a metaphor for the product of a prophet's prophecy. This also applies to leaders of religious organizations, churches, governments—both local and national, and it also applies to you and me. We are known by the product of what we do, plain and simple. Palpatine was creating bad fruit long before he became Emperor, though let's give him some credit for being very sneaky and clandestine. Is the product of your leader's leadership love or hate?

If you are still wondering about your leader, the Emperor's visit to the Death Star brings out three images that are important: separation of church and state, self aggrandizement, and might makes right. These three are clear indications that the fruit is bad. The red guards, the sickly fortune tellers, the military pomp, and the Emperor's attitude all show where he stands. We would be well advised to be mindful of similar imagery in our own leaders.

[53] Dagobah revisited.

Luke sits in Yoda's cave, and Yoda starts reciting the Jedi death chant, "Twilight is upon me . . . ." Yoda pronounces Luke almost a Jedi. One more trial awaits, facing Darth Vader. The Emperor and Yoda both know this must happen. They sense it, feel it, and they also know it from a strategic point of view. The decision Luke must make is how to face Vader. Will he try to kill him? Luke, however, feels the good still inside Vader. How could be possibly justify killing such a person? How we do a thing is just as important as what we do. It is possible to do the right thing in the wrong way, and for the wrong reason. When a disobedient child apologizes, is it valid if he says the apology with indignation, or to avoid punishment, and does not really mean the words? Likewise, if one country invades another country to get rid of a dictator and free the people, is it still right if the liberating country does it for money or for its own political purposes?

Yoda and Ben have limited omniscience into Luke's future, and they have a difficult time believing Luke will do the right thing. Imagine how God must feel about us, even though he has complete omniscience. He knows what we will do and still he lets us do it, even if it is bad for us and removes us from him. That is unfathomable love!

[54] YODA AND LUKE DISCUSS VADER.

Luke asks Yoda if Vader is really his father. Yoda admits that he is, and that he did not expect Vader to reveal that fact to Luke. Then Yoda says that this revelation is unfortunate. "Unfortunate that I know the truth?" Luke responds. Yoda explains to Luke that it is not unfortunate that Luke now knows, but unfortunate because during his initial training on Dagobah, Luke was not ready to handle the temptation to reunite with his father. In so doing Luke risked a major temptation to cross over to the dark side to follow Vader. Yoda tells Luke he had been waiting until Luke's training was complete, so that he could be told this truth when Luke was ready, and in a safer environment.

Yoda realizes that even though Luke survived his first confrontation with Vader, there still exists a seed of temptation to join his father. Luke apologizes for having rushed off without completing his training. He understands now that this as an example of not allowing the Force to flow, and not allowing the timeliness of the Force to work. Luke can now see just how close the Emperor was to capturing him.

As Yoda dies, he reminds Luke for the *nth* time now, to avoid anger, fear, and aggression. Yoda knows that the Emperor will still try to seduce Luke, just as he seduced Anakin, and with the ease in which anger, fear, and aggression make one powerful. As often as Yoda repeats the lesson to avoid anger, fear, and aggression—to include some of his last words as a corporeal body in this scene—it stands as a lesson we can take to heart. We need to keep ourselves from acting out of anger, fearing anything more than God, and preventing ourselves from hostile behavior.

[55] THE GREAT JEDI COMMISSION.

Yoda, still on his deathbed, tells Luke—though Luke has probably already guessed—that when he (Yoda) dies, which is obviously imminent, Luke will be the last of the Jedi Knights. He instructs Luke to, "Pass on what you have learned," and with his dying breath, Yoda informs Luke of another Skywalker. With those last words, Yoda disappears into vapor, somewhat akin to Jesus rising to heaven. Before the ascension of Jesus, the Christ is trying to fit all of the puzzle pieces together, so he gives his followers the Great Commission, as does Yoda to Luke. Jesus basically told his disciples the same thing that Yoda tells his Padawan learner, "Now that you know who I am, pass on what you have learned and experienced."

Jedi must always pass on what they learn. They, and we, are selfish to hold onto knowledge or wisdom that can benefit others. How awesome is the Force anyway! We would want to train Jedi. This is the right way to see the Great Commission. Jesus sending out the apostles, and by extension all of us, can seem daunting. And it can feel as if we are lesser beings, or even disobedient to God, if we do not all become missionaries. Luke was to pass on who he is and what he did, what he knew. We are to pass on who we are, what we do, and what/who we have faith in. Being who we are is the most important part of that commission. Besides just existing in the place where we live, doing what we love is how we are to fulfill The Great Commission. It is inextricably tied to who we are.

Luke does not go proselytizing in the way we are conditioned to think is the right way. Luke is a Jedi, and Luke does the work of a Jedi. This is the right way to understand the Great Commission in our own lives.

[56] . . . FROM A CERTAIN POINT OF VIEW.
LUKE TALKS TO OBI-WAN AFTER YODA'S DEATH.

It seems so relativistic when Obi-Wan only gives Luke the information that, "Darth Vader betrayed and murdered your father" in *Episode IV: A New Hope*. Now, he admits to Luke that when Anakin became Darth Vader, it was as if Anakin betrayed and murdered himself. There is more than a measure of truth in this. Shortly after this interchange, even Vader adamantly proclaims to Luke, "That name no longer has any meaning for me."

Sometimes we also engage in telling half-truths much like Obi-Wan, such as when I tell my son that Santa Claus exists. He does exist in our imaginations, and that is true to a certain way of thinking . . . and it is true that children cannot always handle the full truth of many things. Adults forgetting to recognize simple truths, however, is much more detrimental.

It is important for adults not to lose the ability to be child-like. A child will always become an adult, learn more about the world, and fill in his or her knowledge gaps. It is much more difficult for an adult to continue to believe in the mythological truths of childhood. Adults either never knew some of these truths as children, or they have forgotten them. Santa is not a flesh-and-blood person, but his ethos—the spirit of giving—adults too often forget. Santa is just one example; the others are much more important for adults to recapture. Faith in God is the biggest of these. It is easy to think an omnipresent, omniscient God is simply a silly Sunday school notion when one matures and gains independence. Even many pastors and priests opt for a fictional view of Jesus. Since Jesus archetypes exist in so many other myths, this one can't possibly be real either, they reason. Instead of believing that the unbelievable could actually be true, it is easier to attribute to God all the things you want. For example, in today's world we are stuck in the mud of too much political correctness. We want to please everyone and never say no. If something sounds good, then we believe it. If something sounds bad or non-accepting—non-loving is how it is put—we make our view of God fit that definition. We take a part of the Bible and misquote it to fit the convenience of our lifestyle.

Imagination is the second biggest truth that is true to a certain way of thinking. In many areas of life, it is difficult to be considered mature and taken seriously when you have a desire to use your imagination. Yet, imagination is vital to almost any activity we engage in. In fact, Jesus says,

> "I tell you the truth, anyone who will not receive the kingdom of heaven like a little child will never enter it."
>
> (Luke 18:17)

Following Jesus, believing in him, and reading what he says in the whole Bible is the part of the kingdom of heaven that we can have on earth right now. If we do not accept it unabashedly with a craving imagination, like a child accepts candy, we will never truly know heaven.

The power of imagination is one of those qualities that made Luke Skywalker so powerful. He sees and hears about the temptation of the dark side. At the same time, he feels the good in Vader. He even feels this through the dismal failure of fighting Vader in *Episode V: The Empire Strikes Back*. He must imagine the possibility that Vader can be turned away from the dark side, that Vader is not just twisted and evil as Obi-Wan and Yoda contend. Then Luke cannot just imagine the possibility of Vader's goodness. He is forced to act, and make a decision. The stakes for being right or wrong are enormous, and Luke could have been distracted from his conscious decision of how to best approach Vader. It takes great imagination to see Vader as a person, and even greater imagination to try to save him. Luke calls out the good in Vader. He serves as a prime example of loving his enemies. This is no easy task, and not many of us do it well.

How do we follow Luke's example and love our enemies? Surely, we are not supposed to turn Osama bin Laden to the good side, are we? Osama is a present-day Darth Vader if there ever was one. America once thought him good, the CIA even trained him much like the Jedi council decided to train Anakin. Did Osama then betray us and turn evil, or are we now simply seeing him for what he truly was all along? Do we now see what he truly is? It is difficult for the average American to know where Osama is coming from. What does loving our enemy mean in this scenario? Do we kill bin Laden to give him the dignity of an accountable life? It is hard to know. The question is perhaps most poignant with Saddam Hussein and his on-going trial. In no uncertain terms, he was an evil dictator who most likely would harbor terrorists if it fit his own goals. Certainly, he murdered millions of his own citizens simply for disagreeing with him. The list of atrocities goes on. And yet, he is receiving a dignified trial. To Saddam, the trial must seem rather foolish. Of course, a tyrant is bound to see any love as ridiculous, be it in the form of a trial or any other gesture. Is there anything from the life of Jesus that would help us understand how to treat Saddam?

[57] FEELINGS. AS IN, NOTHING MORE THAN.

In *Episode IV: A New Hope*, Obi-Wan tells Luke to stretch out with his feelings, to trust his feelings, because his eyes might betray him. In *Episode V: The Empire Strikes Back*, Yoda instructs Luke to feel the Force around him, flowing through him and through everything. When Luke guesses that Leia is his sister, however, Obi-Wan tells him to bury his feelings deep down, that they served Luke well, but that they could be made to also serve the Emperor!

It would have been a good and balanced thing for the dialogue in *Star Wars* to include as much about thinking as it does about feeling. Feelings, though, seem to be the thing we need to be in touch with these days, and feelings come from the heart. The western world has really majored in workings of the head, so this trend, however unbalanced, is refreshing. At least it is a small acknowledgment that the heart is important, and how it is not always healthy to ignore our feelings. Feelings are valuable, and the practice of recognizing them strengthens our intuition, which is an important feminine trait in a Jedi's life. Going too far can be dangerous, though, and we see feelings out of balance with though that get in the way and lead to the dark side . . . especially when relationships are involved. In *Episode V: The Empire Strikes Back*, when Han and Leia and Chewy and C-3PO are heading into a trap in Cloud City, they are the emotional bait that Darth Vader uses to lure Luke. Luke's feelings cloud his judgment as he travels to Cloud City. Then, in the last scenes of *Episode VI: Return of the Jedi*, Vader senses Luke's thoughts about Leia and uses this information to taunt Luke into fighting.

This is a great lesson for us to learn. We can automatically assume that when it comes to the people we love, our feelings are very highly charged. If we tell ourselves this ahead of time, when it comes time to deal with people we love in stressful situations, we can do better in the interchange by already understanding that we tend to be unbalanced and see things unclearly. Acting on this, we can reach a better conclusion and give ourselves space before reacting harshly or overdramatically . . . and certainly not violently. The prime example of feelings going too far, and thinking going too little, is in the destructive adolescent relationship between Anakin and Padmé in *Episodes II* and *III*. On their exile to Naboo, Padmé entreats Anakin to follow his thoughts about their being together to the logical conclusion. Her words are, of course, unconvincing because she speaks them as the two are on a romantic island in Naboo. They have just shared a romantic dinner together, and are now in an intimate, dimly-lit room in front of a fireplace. Finally, she is wearing tight, black leather! They both allow their feelings to rule and leave logic behind completely. This selfishness leads to an unhealthy relationship, lies, unnecessary pain, and the repercussions of their relationship speed the decline of an entire civilization.

[58] Separating the wheat from the chaff. General Solo and General Calrissian bid each other good luck.

When we meet Han Solo, it does not seem that he glories in the base human degradation which is par for Jabba the Hutt and company, yet Han does owe Jabba money for dumping a load of cargo that he was smuggling. In short, they are business associates after a fashion. More important than their business relationship, Han shares a similar philosophy with Jabba. He believes in a "bunch of luck and nonesuch" and "hokey weapons and ancient religions are no match for a good blaster at your side." Through the film series, Han shakes off much of this cavalier nature, but despite the civilizing influences of Princess Leia and the Rebel Alliance, Han is still widely known throughout the galaxy as a wild and individualistic character. There are numerous times when evidence of this comes out. One such time is when Han says, "Good luck" when responding to "May the Force be with you!" from the like-minded Lando Calrissian, even though both men are now serving as generals with the Rebel Alliance. This exchange takes place just as Han and Lando are departing on their separate missions in *Episode VI: Return of the Jedi*.

Is Han Solo the wheat or the chaff in the biblical sense of believing in Christ truly or simply going along for the ride? Does Han believe in the Force or does he simply find a lucrative place to be for a while? If Han Solo is a little shy about saying, "May the Force be with you," this is understandable. Church jargon can be the same way. Perhaps Han understands the gravity of his words. Invoking the Force, just as we invoke the Lord and God, can begin to seem a little odd when overused. Even though listening to, talking with, and worshipping God on a daily basis is a good thing . . . he is holy and terribly powerful after all, and holy is not as common as dishwasher liquid, so a measure of restraint is good. Han might hold off talking about the Force for just those reasons.

Where he comes from, however, makes the issue suspect. The philosophy of his past is a go-with-the-flow, stick-with-the-best-thing-you-come-across kind of thought pattern. Han does not go off to find the Rebels because he is passionate about their cause. He almost accidentally becomes a hero, and he might have been sticking around the Rebel Alliance because it is the best opportunity to cross his path. The truth is we cannot know; just as we cannot know if a person is going to live for eternity or not. In many church traditions, it is easy for people to attend and not particularly believe. Maybe they go because it is the best thing that has come along. Maybe Han and Lando just have good intentions and their hearts are good. Does this mean they believe? On the surface, they do seem like believers. Perhaps the Force, like God, is the only one able to judge the heart.

[59] THE EMPEROR'S INTEGRITY.
VADER AND THE EMPEROR DISCUSS LUKE'S ARRIVAL ON THE FOREST MOON OF ENDOR.

When Darth Vader returns to the Emperor to inform him that Luke is part of the Rebel Alliance landing party on Endor's forest moon, the Emperor doubts him, saying "Are you sure?" and "Strange that I have not (sensed that)," and finally, "I wonder if your feelings are quite clear on this matter." Darth Vader assures him they are, and the Emperor then retorts, "Go down to the moon and wait. He will come to you. I have foreseen it." Vader must have wanted to call foul. Can't you hear him say, "What? You foresaw it just now? Just a second ago you doubted me, now you not only agree, but you have foreseen him coming to me . . . why didn't you foresee him on the moon or in the spaceship?"

But this is the double talk you get when you serve an evil master who is just as concerned with his own image as being seen as the most powerful, most filled with foresight, most everything. This reminds me of one of my former bosses. Whenever we talked, it was as if he had an issue with being wrong. When I pointed something out, or even suggested a more efficient course of action, he would sometimes want me to do it the wrong or inefficient way just to prove that he was more powerful.

None of us actually thinks the exaggerated and gloriously evil Emperor is not a duplicitous, egomaniacal, lying heap of Sith. However, we know the reality of this situation in bosses and politicians, religious leaders, etc. The Emperor is deliciously evil, as in he is fun to watch, as long as he stays inside my television screen.

[60] THOSE ADORABLE, LITTLE THIRD-WORLD EWOKS.

Which came first, the Ewok ride at Disneyland or the Ewoks? Is there even such a ride? At any rate, there is no doubt the Ewoks serve a primarily cuddly commercial purpose.

The facts remain: the Empire ignores the Ewoks, who play a major role in defeating the Empire's base on Endor. This allows Han to destroy the Empire's shield generator, which leads to destruction of the Empire's nearly completed Death Star II, and ultimately to the downfall of the entire Empire. This is a wonderful story and an excellent example of an impossible victory by the insignificant underdog. The Rebels actually take time to get to know the Ewoks. Han and Luke and the whole gang do not need to allow themselves to be taken prisoner by the Ewoks. They could just as easily shoot them or escape and go on with their vitally important mission. Luke steadies Han and simply remains observant to what happens during their capture. He interferes just a little at just the right moment, and the result is they find Leia, obtain supplies, and gain the aid of an unexpectedly resilient tribe of allies. This is an example of the Taoist concept of *wu wei*; Han and Luke let the Force flow, or allow God's grace in the situation to flow (my thought, not Taoist, and as always these are not exactly parallel concepts). Even C-3PO overcomes his seeming inability to tell stories from *Episode IV: A New Hope* to being a conveyor of verbal tradition as he recounts the Rebel band's victory to the Ewoks.

It seems third-world countries, much like the Ewoks, are often ignored until they are worth something of political or economic value. It would be Christ-like for us to help them before we help ourselves. This is not to say that we should halt all domestic plans to help the poor and the sick. However, we already have so much, including many of the answers to problems faced by many third-world countries. Sure, helping others creates many more issues and problems. It's just that these countries and people need our help, and the fact that they need our help makes our inaction and ignorance of their plight that much more important. There is truth to myth stories. Much like the Ewoks' assistance of the Rebel Alliance in ways that they could hardly imagine, if we help the third-world countries in a significant and meaningful way, the biggest surprise may well be their ability to help us in ways that we could never imagine.

[61] VADER'S ADMISSION.

Scene: Luke knows that Vader can sense his presence on Endor, and Luke gives himself up not only to provide a diversion for the Rebels, but also to confront Vader. They meet in a passageway, and Vader informs Luke that the Emperor is expecting him.

Luke — "I know, Father."

Vader — "So, you have accepted the truth."

Luke — "I've accepted the truth that you were once Anakin Skywalker, my father."

Vader — "That name no longer has any meaning for me."

Luke — "It is the name of your true self. You've only forgotten. I know there is good in you. The Emperor hasn't driven it from you fully. That is why you couldn't destroy me. That's why you won't bring me to your Emperor now."

Vader — "I see you have constructed a new lightsaber."

Vader — "Your skills are complete. Indeed, you are powerful, as the Emperor has foreseen.

They stand for a moment, Luke's weapon in the hands of Vader, dangerously close to touching him. Vader extinguishes the lightsaber.

Luke — "Come with me."

Vader — "Obi-Wan once thought as you do."

Vader — "You don't know the power of the dark side. I must obey my master."

Luke — "I will not turn . . . and you'll be forced to kill me."

Vader — "If that is your destiny."

Luke — "Search your feelings, Father. You can't do this. I feel the conflict within you. Let go of your hate."

Vader — "It is too late for me, son. The Emperor will show you the true nature of the Force. He is your master now."

Luke   —   "Then my father is truly dead."

Episode VI: The Return of the Jedi

Luke receives Ben and Yoda's advice regarding Vader. Still, he dis-obeys in that he knows he feels the good in Vader and that he must confront his father with this truth. This is my wife's favorite scene in the whole series. She loves the beauty of Vader's sad admission to Luke that it is too late—Vader clearly shows his regret. David Prowse, the actor inside the Vader costume, does an excellent job in acting out these emotions with just the movements of the Vader mask and costume.

Luke figures that Vader wants to be with him more than almost anything. Remember in *Episode V: The Empire Strikes Back* when Va-der says that Obi-Wan is wise to hide Luke from him? Luke uses this knowledge. Vader's pauses in the dialogue above demonstrates that he really does consider what Luke is saying. Vader does not want Luke to end up saying "My father is truly dead," and yet he does not want to admit that he is still Anakin Skywalker. Truly there is conflict within him. Luke lays it on the line and tells Vader he will not turn and that Vader himself must kill him. Just as Luke does not want to kill Vader, he knows that Vader does not want to kill him. He feels affection in Vader.

What seems so explicitly Christian here is that Luke uses the phrase, "That is the name of your true self." We all have true selves, and in this world, we are a little Vader and a little Yoda all at the same time. For us, it is not a life of either light or dark. We do good things and we sin, most likely all in the same day, every day. We have a true self that God is calling out of us. I love this because often I do not feel worthy of God's affection, but I do feel a true self in me that knows how not to sin and how to do things right. I want to give this gift to God and to myself. Of course, the dark side is easier. This is the way of the world. It is also true, though, that even the worst person ever must work hard against the pull to get rid of original and continual sin. What a strange paradox that we can't help doing wrong things but we keep wanting not to. This is part of the longing we find in the double sunset on Tatooine when we hear that lilting melody. This is a self that the Force helps us move toward in this life. This true self does not sin, is confident, poised, smart, healthy, selfless, loving, humble, strong-willed, big-hearted, pure . . . this true self is like a Jedi.

Vader feels the temptation to join Luke. He is probably thinking of how he would like to be with his son, establish a relationship, learn about his life, how it was Luke was even born and find out if Padmé is still alive. He probably wants to talk about all the things they have in common. Vader probably wants to be a dad. However, fear takes control of him. He must wonder whether the Emperor knows anything about this temptation. Does the Emperor even feel a tremor in the Force when Darth Vader considers this option? Thinking of all the ramifications of turning back to the good seems to scare Vader, who beckons to the guards to come in and take Luke away. Perhaps when he feels this knotted fear, he tells Luke that the Emperor will teach Luke the true nature of the Force.

Luke then removes the attention and affection Vader cherishes and says the one thing Vader most wants to avoid hearing, "Then my father is truly dead." Those words strike Vader, and might be part of the persuasion by the light side of the Force that causes Vader to save Luke's life at the end.

A final admission that shows the power of good welling up in Vader happens when he turns, of course, but it is noteworthy that with his last breath, Anakin—no longer Darth Vader—wants Luke to take the mask off Vader's own face so that he "can look on you [Luke] with my own eyes." He wants his true self to see Luke, and to be seen by Luke.

[62] "In time, you will call me Master."

It is eternally and universally important whom we call Master, and both God and Satan want us to call them by that name and put them in that position in our lives. Of course, there are lesser masters that we opt for all the time. Even while we believe we are chosen, or God's people, or on the right path, we are often deceived or distracted into putting most of our effort, desire, and love into a lesser master. That thing becomes an idol. Even if you say you belong to God, you may not be practicing the act of belonging to God.

Jesus said,

> "No one can serve two masters. Either he will hate the one and love the other, or he will be devoted to the one and despise the other. You cannot serve both God and Money."
>
> (Matthew 6:24)

This is just a fact. Money, in this context, is the lesser master, though we could certainly substitute others. Luke could not be a Jedi and a Sith.

However, Luke has no respect for the Emperor's dark devices. He comes right out and says, "Your overconfidence is your weakness." Gutsy! Vader even looks at him as if to say, "What did you dare say to the most powerful person in the universe?" Then the Emperor taunts Luke with information that his friends are flying into a trap, and that everything is happening according to his grand design.

Note to readers with evil Emperor-types in their lives: Do not listen to a deceiver. They will mix truth with lies every time. You get as far away from these types of people as possible.

Notice how the Emperor eggs Luke on. He goads Luke that the young Jedi is "mistaken about a great many things," and calls Luke and the Rebel Alliance's efforts an "insignificant rebellion." This is a pattern: The Emperor alternately puts Luke down, then is kind; he distracts Luke, then he engages him. His goal always is to keep Luke off balance, make Luke doubt what he knows, then extract a response. At times, the Emperor is even quiet, but never calm.

Inside, he rages and hates. The Emperor does not coax Luke to join with him, there is no invitation to "please join us." He pushes Luke to say, "No!" with all his might, and in the aggression of saying no with full force, the Emperor knows he may get Luke to say, "No!" with the emotions of anger, fear, and aggression. If so, Luke will be easy prey for enticement to the dark side by the ease with which he can garner power. However, this is the power of the world, and not the power of meekness that Jesus used.

In real life, there are even more subtleties to the dark side that are designed solely to take us off the pure path. An excellent resource for identifying these distractions is the book of Proverbs in the Bible. As with all the books of the Bible, they are not helpful just to Christians, they are helpful to people of any religion.

We all serve masters, whether we like to admit this or not. Since we are small, frail beings whose days are numbered, what do any of us matter in the grand scheme of the universe? Why does it matter who we serve in our life? Does it really matter?

The Old and New Testaments seem to indicate that there is something forever important about what we, insignificant though we are, do with our bodies. Whom we call master resonates in this life in the form of history. Who, what, and how we live our lives does change things. More than that, these Old and New Testaments seem to indicate that we are judged for what our bodies do in this life. It is not as if a Hitler can be a Hitler in this life and then just so easily turn around once his body dies and say, "Just kidding, I'm really not that kind of person at all."

The excuse that some use, that we don't have a master, is also an interesting one. At first, Han Solo does not believe that he serves any master. "There's no mystical energy field that controls my destiny," Han says with his customary bravado. He believes in self, as his last name implies. However, having yourself as a master is having a master. If we are able to maintain any sense of reality, we know we are not very good masters of ourselves. Look what trouble Han gets himself into. The only way to keep this philosophy and avoid not doing what we want to do is to not want to do anything; and that is not only impossible, but un-fulfilling and unbalanced.

Yoda's presence, his devotion to things other than himself, and his giving of himself causes Luke to call him Master. Yoda allows Luke to freely choose him and freely unchoose him, just as the Trinity God allows us to do the same. Vader and the Emperor, however, use brute force and deception. Vader says, "You don't know the power of the dark side of the Force. I must obey my master." They use anger, fear, and aggression in an attempt to persuade Luke to come over to the dark side.

[63] THE WAY LOVE WINS.
"YOU HAVE FAILED, YOUR HIGHNESS.
I AM A JEDI KNIGHT, LIKE MY FATHER BEFORE ME."

There is no person alive who does not have a weakness for one part of the dark side or the other. Whether it be power politics, spiritual or supernatural power, material wealth, or any number of obsessions from the Christian churches . . . we all want power of some sort, and many times we fall for the easy power that does not take faith to possess.

The way love wins takes faith. Luke is victorious at the end of *Episode VI: Return of the Jedi*. He marks a triumphant return by the Jedi Knights. He defeats Darth Vader and he throws down his lightsaber. He refuses to take what seems like success and murder Vader. Instead, Luke stubbornly refuses this minor victory in which he likely will end up as the lucrative second-in-command to the Emperor, which would be no victory at all. Instead he stands up tall to the Emperor. "You have failed, your highness. I am a Jedi, like my father before me." Just as in *Episode V: The Empire Strikes Back*, Luke gives up his life. Why would Luke do this?

It may seem a random connection, but Luke's action shows that he has learned a lesson that in our world is exemplified in the parable of the vine and the branches, John 15. This is where God prunes the vines, as in he shapes his creation, and this might mean ending our lives or limiting our successes in order to prune us if we do not work for his glory. In this passage, Jesus does not necessarily seem concerned with the length or quality of our life. We, on the other hand, tend to be rather concerned about both. We read these verses and we don't want to be pruned. Our first instinct is to preserve and prolong life, at whatever cost. Jesus is concerned with the fruit of our lives. That is, how much do we love him and each other in whatever time we do have to live. It is good to fear God and his power over us. However, in this passage, I think fearing God is not the main lesson. I think the point here is to focus on living by the Spirit, like using the Force, to be fruitful.

In this moment when Vader is beaten down and the Emperor starts laughing and shows pleasure at Luke's abilities to harness the Force, the symbol of Vader's mechanical hand brings Luke back from the edge of rage. He suddenly comprehends that his own mechanical hand represents two very different and powerful forces. Luke's mechanical hand is the direct result of the nature of the dark side. In *Episode V: The Empire Strikes Back*, Luke confronts a ghostly, dream-world Vader who was also himself. This hand, however, is actual, tangible evidence that he is just like his father, and he connects this with the dark side. Second, the action of Luke slicing off his father's hand reminds Luke that Vader cut off Luke's hand . . . instead of taking his life. Vader showed Luke grace, therefore Luke decides to show grace back to his father. In his giving of grace, refusing the anger, fear, and aggression, Luke truly becomes a Jedi Knight. Metaphorically, this is the fruitfulness that God wants out of us, as part of himself, as part of the vine. This is the ultimate image of overcoming evil with good (Romans 12:21).

Perhaps Luke underestimates the light side. It is ironic, this truth: that Luke's single act of sparing Vader turns the tables on the entire *Star Wars* universe. Before Luke is born, it was thought that Anakin Skywalker was to fulfill the prophesy and restore balance to the Force, which meant that he was to find the Sith Lord and kill him. In the prequels, the Jedi masters do not at first understand what restoring the balance means, as they themselves are not even aware of a dark Sith Lord. In *Episode III: Revenge of the Sith*, Anakin has the opportunity to strike down the Emperor and fulfill his destiny. He fails and instead becomes evil. Luke's sacrifice helps turn Anakin back to his original course, who with the last ounce of his life, thrusts the Emperor down the shaft to kill him. Were there a God in this *Star Wars* universe, Vader's action in this instance would be due to Luke living for God, and demonstrating evidence that the Holy Spirit is truly with him.

[64] FIGHTING WITH OUR SOULS. THE HORN BLAST OF THE EWOKS.

The climax and turning point in the battle on the forest moon of Endor happens when the Ewoks sound their trumpets everywhere in the forest to signal an attack on the Imperial stormtroopers. Like horns in the battle of Jericho or Gideon's torches and shouts during his battle against the Midianites, an insignificant band of hardly warriors—the Ewoks—thinly surrounds on oppressive, overwhelmingly powerful enemy of stormtroopers, and with all their might, with all that is in their little bodies and souls, they cry out against evil. These shouts of the soul strike fear into the hearts of any enemy.

[65] It's all in the uniform.

What do white stormtroopers in dense green jungle, British red coats in brown and green American fields, and American desert camouflage in Baghdad City have in common? They are the uniforms of empires, and as such are an important part of warfare. To wear a military uniform is dignified, and soldiers are right to take pride in their uniforms. However, the question is sometimes, would you rather be proud and dead, or use your clothing to confuse your enemy and remain alive? There is a time to wear a uniform, and there is a time not to. An Empire with many exalted and important people often dictates a proud and forceful appearance. Blasting a white stormtrooper in a green jungle, shooting a red coat just about anywhere, or targeting a soldier in desert camouflage in the midst of a city is pretty easy. In *Episode III: Revenge of the Sith*, the early Empire does try to match uniforms to the surroundings just a little. It remains true, however, that one of the qualities of an empire is garish uniformity, especially in the dress of the soldiers. Sadly, this represents placement of a greater importance on how a soldier looks than the individual's life inside the uniform.

[66] DEATH FOR KIDS.

Although ultimately commercial in nature, we ought not overlook the value of the cuddly Ewoks. In one battle sequence, when two little Ewoks are fighting side by side, one is blasted by an Imperial scout-walker and both Ewoks fall down. The live one stands up and tries to get the other Ewok up only to realize that he is dead. He then moans and cries for him. This scene is death for kids. The death of that one tiny Ewok becomes more real to young audiences than the deaths of hundreds of adult characters.

As silly as it might seem, little kids identify with little teddy bears more than they do with adults. An Ewok even moves like a toddler. When one of the Ewoks dies, a child learns more about good and evil than in perhaps all the other movies combined. Children love Ewoks, and they learn what it is like to lose a loved one when one of the furry little creatures dies. As commercial as some of Lucas' creatures are, he also intends them to help small children understand the lessons of myth, and they do so with great power.

If the symbolism does something for you, as well, you may find it interesting to note that the harsh versus the precious, the hard versus the fluffy, is also one of the motifs of myth that Joseph Campbell talks about (*Myth*, Campbell/Moyers).

[67] JEDI FIGHTING.

Jedi fighting, as evidenced in the last battle between Vader and Luke, uses more than just lightsaber swordplay. Luke bounds and somersaults out of Vader's grasp. They also use ideological arguments. "I will not fight you," Luke says, taunting Vader with their father-son relationship. They search each other's thoughts, "I feel the conflict in you, let go of the hate," we hear from Luke, "Your thoughts betray you," both Vader and Luke say at various times, and Vader says near the end, "If you won't turn, perhaps she (Leia) will." They are like opposing nations that find out all they can about each other, who their friends are, who their siblings are, what each other may be hiding.

It is Vader's taunting Luke about going after Leia that finally sets Luke off. The Emperor is pleased with Luke's dominance. He thinks Luke was using his hate to grow stronger. However, Luke is not dominating out of rage, but out of a righteous anger. He fights out of love and defense for Leia. The Emperor fails to understand that the difference between rage and righteous anger is love. Many people in America today do not want to read the Bible enough to understand that God sometimes gets angry and kills people who do things against him. God is not just the all-accepting, warm, fuzzy, politically correct God that they pick and choose him to be. This knowledge does not change our love for those with whom God is angry. How could we even determine who those people are? And, contrary to the belief of terrorists and mobs, we are not God's weapon.

There is a temptation in our world today to believe that evil does not really exist, therefore fighting is never really necessary. This is just a very effective Sith tactic of misinformation. You don't need to be a war monger to believe that some wars must be fought. Like Luke and Vader posturing, many wars are ideological. For example, we have the radical Islamic influence—eastern extremists—and the radical fundamentalist movements—western extremists. By not fighting these extremist fundamentals, we allow them to win. Is the kind of fighting America is doing in Iraq right now Jedi fighting? Are we showing extremists or their potential recruits that they are not following the tenets of their own systems of belief? A Jedi fights with all of who he or she is, the whole person. Are we using one of the most powerful weapons of the light side—rationality—together with a giving, warm, and open heart? We could die only fighting with power, or we could die giving ourselves to the freedom of Iraq by fighting with all that we are, just like the Jedi.

[68] THE WORLD REJOICES.

After the Death Star II blows up, there is a grand celebration. Everyone is happy and joyful that the days of the Empire's rule are over. Parties on all the major *Star Wars* planets are shown, and the unfortunate pan-world happy music replaces the Ewok "chub chub" tune. This is the Lucasfilm version of heaven, it seems, and though it lacks a grand repentance of everyone's part in allowing the Empire to exist, the idea of the worlds' rejoicing is a true image. Our hearts desire this celebration of good over evil following the final battle. It is a reminder of the very hope we have in the new Jerusalem of Christ's return and the final conquering of the devil. When Jesus comes back, there will be no ambiguity about his return. What is good and right and true will be quite clear. The images in the last scenes of *Episode VI: Return of the Jedi* are at least heading in the right direction.

The party at the end of time, similar to the universal party here depicted, will be a magnified version of what can be experienced in the truest forms of corporate worship. There is music, teaching, praying, creeds, and communion. It is important for the words to be precise and thorough in their form and theology, the music must be capable of reaching the congregation, prayer must encompass the elements of the Lord's Prayer, and there must be a remembrance of Christ's sacrifice in communion. It is all a purifying process. Since God is light and in him there is no darkness at all, getting closer to God through the above experience illumines the sin in our lives. We become aware of it, we repent, and this allows us to worship more fully. If we don't repent, our spirits cannot go forward. Our bodies remain in the same places they otherwise would be; just not as much happens to us in the larger sense of resurrection. When this true worship experience happens, there are moments—usually during singing—when a precious energy courses through the congregation that seems more than just a sum of the power of the moment. Other events that come close to this emotionally and spiritually are sporting events, or at the concert of a great band, or at a political rally. The commonality is unity of purpose in an impassioned environment. The difference with worship, however, it is as tender as it is forceful, as quiet as it is loud, as permanent as it is fleeting, as selfless as it encourages individually, and as present of the mind as it is letting go of our conscious selves. My mouth forms the shape of the word *holy* to describe it. It feels as if God's holy presence is more fully among all of us for that period of time than at any other moment. This is a fraction of what God's party at the end of time will be like.

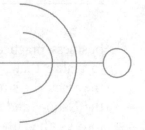

EPISODE I
THE PHANTOM MENACE

[69] HOW TO DISCOVER THINGS
FROM A MID-LEVEL BAD GUY.

Obi-Wan Kenobi and Qui-Gon Jin approach a mass of spaceships encircling a planet in the first scenes of *Episode I: The Phantom Menace*. They request permission to land in the main station immediately. The Trade Federation responds "Of course," and, "As you know, our operation is perfectly legal." When working with a mid- to low-level bad guy, one that is not so savvy, just observe and listen. In this example and others in the first few minutes of this first prequel of a movie, the Trade Federation representatives point right to the issue, right to their fear, and right to their crime. This is another way in which *Star Wars* helps develop a viewer's common sense.

The Trade Federation is concerned about the legality of its presence. In fact, we learn later in the movie that what they are doing is legally very dubious. Next, they try to kill the Jedi ambassadors straight away, without even talking to them. Darth Sidious/Senator Palpatine prompts them to do this, but it does not take much convincing on his part. In conversations with each other, the Trade Federation representatives fear the Jedi because they fear the power that the Jedi might exercise over them. Again, the mid-to low-level bad guy points to exactly the tactics that he so fears—his own. They fear brute force because they are about to use it. Everyone knows about the Jedi, that the Jedi Knights work for peace and do not make people do things. The Viceroy's fear of brute force clouds his judgment to this knowledge, even though its realization could help them either in their evil pursuits or to see through the lies of Palpatine. Instead, the Trade Federation only interprets the actions of others through this lens of fear and force. They are mostly greedy, and this greed causes moral ambiguity, back-handed business practices, and weak-mindedness. Even when they come to realize that they are being used as puppets by the Dark Lord, they lack the strength of character to break these ties, apologize to the Naboo, and enlist the help of the Republic in dealing with evil forces—the Sith—with whom they have struck a deal. Pride causes the death of many on both sides in the ensuing battle.

Obi-Wan intuits a little of this as soon as he walks into the waiting room on the Trade Federation's blockade station. He tells Qui-Gon, "I have a bad feeling about this," then adds, "It's not about the mission, master, it's something elsewhere . . . elusive . . . ."

Qui-Gon responds that he should not center his focus on these anxieties, but rather keep his full attention on the here and the now. But Yoda had told Obi-Wan to be mindful of the future, Obi-Wan responds. To this Qui-Gon corrects, "But not at the expense of the moment. Be mindful of the living Force, my young Padawan."

Qui-Gon teaches Obi-Wan to learn that to understand a situation he must not ignore the living Force. For us, this is like learning to discern a direction in which the Holy Spirit might be leading us, or how we receive council from God. In so doing, we observe and listen, just as Qui-Gon and Obi-Wan do when they discovered that the Trade Federation consists of some mid-level bad guys, though the Jedi do not use those terms. If Qui-Gon pursued and encouraged the nugget of truth in Obi-Wan's feelings, they might have discovered sooner the evil intention's behind the Trade Federation's blockade.

Maybe God gives us our daily bread, our daily energy, and the direction we need for just right now . . . and these we are to use to do what he wants us to do in a day. Maybe living in a faithful way means having faith in the future he brings to us, the information with which we are presented, as the Jedi in these scenes quickly discover. Maybe he knows that if we only focus on looking away at a future we can only guess at, as Obi-Wan maybe is doing, we somehow become less powerful.

[70] THE NABOO NAIVETÉ

In *Episode I: The Phantom Menace*, Lucas and company parody ideologies that are not fully thought out, even perhaps only half-baked. The Trade Federation is half-bad. They either do not understand or do not care enough that their greed makes them bad. They end up being tools for the evil purposes of Darth Sidious. The Naboo, on the other hand, are half-good.

They naively believe that they are living in a peaceful way, as symbolized in the choice of the Naboo to elect young, idealistic queens and senators to rule them. It was in this state of supposed peace that the Trade Federation blocks their out-going and in-coming commerce, easily kills the citizens, and without one shot fired, takes over the planet, destroying much of their nature and wildlife in the process. Contrast this to the Jedi belief of using the Force for knowledge and defense. Knowledge in using thinking skills and intelligence gathering, common sense, and intuition would easily demonstrate to the Naboo that they need more than good-will to maintain their lifestyle. Defense would have served the Naboo well. It is hard to disrespect a person or a nation when that person or that nation is respecting its own borders. If a person or a nation has a defense against violence, that person or nation is much less likely to have people or groups act violently towards them. The Naboo do not respect the ability of practically any group to take away what they hold dear until all their freedoms are whisked away. They are a microcosm of the entire Republic who, although they employ the Jedi as peace-keepers, get into trouble in the prequels through an inability to defend themselves against an opposing army.

If Naboo is an exaggerated condition of the Republic, then Amidala is their poster child. She buys into a deception that spins her around and makes her as culpable as Anakin for the ascendancy of the Empire. Palpatine is the dark Sith Lord Darth Sidious, soon to become the Emperor. Politically, he starts out as just a senator from Naboo. He appeals to the greed of the Trade Federation, then pits them against his home planet, knowing full well the Naboo weakness for naiveté. He even takes the temporary set-back of Queen

Amidala's escape to Coruscant, where he and the senate reside and work, and manipulates her into thinking that their biggest advocate, the Supreme Chancellor Valorum, is the weakest link in their pursuit of freedom. Valorum is, no doubt, bogged down in the red tape that Palpatine sets in place, then Palpatine convinces Queen Amidala to make an impassioned speech that results in the removal from power of Supreme Chancellor Valorum on Amidala's call for a vote of no confidence. In her idealistic state, Palpatine tells Queen Amidala a half-truth to deceive her into choosing the seeming lesser of two evils, and of course, he only presents her with two bad options. This is the same tactic he later uses with Anakin.

The foolishness of Amidala and the Naboo is a metaphor for a glaring error of the 1980s, though this movie obviously did not come out in that decade. The '80s was the epitome of a "trust children and follow the wisdom of kids" phase in our history. This is not the same as having childlike faith. It even led to a few sexual harassment cases where adults were put into jail because of the developmental incapacities of children were lauded as truth and admitted as evidence in the courtroom. We learned the very hard way, as Amidala's mistakes also illustrate, that youth, by its very nature, lacks wisdom. Art does not have to have a message to it, but when it does have a message that points to truth, we need to learn to recognize that message and allow it to inform the way we live, as this movie reveals to us. In the western world, we have a long tradition of learning through science and thought. Part of the popularity of *Star Wars* is our collective desire to also learn from story and myth.

[71] DON'T JEDI KNIGHTS EVER GET THE HOT SWEATS? OBI-WAN KENOBI AND QUI-GON JINN ON NABOO.

When you are led in a completely pointless direction, say into the watery core of a planet, and a droid army is tightening its grip on the planet with every second, and you get lost in this watery core . . . don't you just get those panic sweats? Despite all their use of the Force and their training and everything, when a Jedi actually makes a mistake somewhere along the line, misreads the direction one is supposed to take, second-guesses or third-guesses himself, then realizes that he has botched the job and perhaps thousands of people are dying because his party is lost in this watery planet core with no idea how to get out . . .! Would it hurt to have the Jedi sweat and be unsure of themselves every once in a while, then resort to meditation or some other ritual of calming to get rational again? Jedi Knights are highly trained, we know. But when normal people find themselves in such situations, well, maybe not these exact situations, it would help us learn what to do if we could just see the Jedi as a bit more human.

Qui-Gon and Obi-Wan do get lost, and Qui-Gon's response is, "the Force will show us the way." Confusion and frustration are difficult to deal with, much harder at times than a duel with lightsabers. At least in a duel you know what is the goal. Qui-Gon's abundance of faith is disturbing . . . or, at least, a little simplistic. He might well be as strong and faithful as he seems, but Jedi are human, too, and a little slip up and readjustment would help us to imagine how we might respond to failure or to getting lost—either literally or figuratively. These are the times we need faith the most. What would it look like to see a Jedi using the Force in that situation? Perhaps he would just stop, breathe, re-focus, remind himself that the Force is with him, ask the Force to help him find the way, sing a little praise song to himself, and then listen to hear the Force's direction.

[72] Evil wants to be legitimate.

The Trade Federation, the half-bad guys, desperately desire to be seen as legitimate. When Nute Gunray, one of the ugly Trade Federation leaders, talks with his new prisoners Sio Bibble, Queen Amidala, and Captain Panaka, he wants them to sign a treaty that will, in his words, "legitimize our occupation." Again, these words unconsciously point directly to one of the Trade Federation's largest vulnerabilities, the fact that they are not legitimate. Darth Sidious assures the Trade Federation that the Republic will not discover even the smallest bit of the truth, but still they fear that the truth will get out. They are right to do so. Truth always finds a way.

As we see in the graphic metaphor of the ride through the planet's core, each big fish is eaten by an even bigger fish. This repeated image is a direct metaphor for what is happening on the surface of Naboo, and in the space surrounding Naboo. One big fish is eating another. The Trade Federation is a big fish that wants the leadership of Naboo—considered by all to be a small fish—to sign a document stating that the Trade Federation's occupation by force is fair. This lends further legitimacy to the illegal trade blockade put on by the Trade Federation. In like fashion, an even more powerful fish—the Sith Lords, Darth Sidious and Darth Maul—need the Trade Federation as a legitimate front for the chaos they want to bring about. Recognizing patterns that can point to either good or bad relationships is a big part of intuition and wisdom.

Many of us tend to want to just believe someone who tells us something. That is a bad pattern, always. Being suspicious and untrusting takes it too far the other direction. Being even and questioning is a good, balanced way to be. For example: do you just give money to some charity that shows pictures on TV of starving kids in Africa? That is hardly responsible. We must always research the organizations, research the problems. Throwing money at problems is not a very good response. Being involved as a person is a great thing. Since this section is about evil desiring legitimacy, are there organizations that take your money in order to show a legitimate front? My favorite area in which to see this is in televangelism. Some of the hosts are sitting in plush, completely over-decorated, posh surroundings and they talk about God's work. If the almighty God, who created gold and silver, himself came down as a man of lowly status, do you not have cause to suspect the big-haired, caked make-up, finely-clothed hosts of many of those shows? At least you know where quite a bit of the money is going!

To recognize the patterns of evil, or even of mediocrity, is like a preemptive strike . . . like the Jedi's ability to see things before they happen.

[73] THE PARADOX OF WARRIORS
BEING AGENTS OF PEACE.

In *Episode I: The Phantom Menace*, as in all the other *Star Wars* movies, the Jedi Knights are supposed to be agents of peace, and this is at times hard to reconcile. "Thou shall not murder," is a commandment, after all. However, the Jedi seem unable to get through two consecutive scenes without killing someone. The Old Testament is where God seems to do all the killing, and there is a general impression that in the New Testament Jesus showed us what true love is like and that killing people is no longer something he is involved in. This is not exactly true. In Acts, God kills Ananias and Sapphira just for lying. They don't even get a trial or a warning, not even jail time, just *boom*, they are dead.

God killing people and people killing people are two different things, though. He judges the heart, we cannot. What are we then to think about the Jedi's tendency to use violence in the name of and in the pursuit of peace? Even the Sith use this excuse. Is this another of myth's extreme cases to show us that peace is something for which we must fight? How they fight is important to the answer. The Jedi never just go out and fight for the sake of fighting. It is always purposeful. In the first *Star Wars* trilogy, the two sides are clearly defined as good and evil, so their purpose is not at all ambiguous. Luke joins the Rebel Forces and is an asset to their military. In the prequels, evil works behind the scenes. The established good side is dominant, so the altruistic reasons for fighting and killing are somewhat more opaque. It is easy to see the ills of a dominant force. Qui-Gon and Obi-Wan guard Queen Amidala, but do not fight a battle for her. However, they are heavily involved in the fighting and planning, so where do they draw the line? These two Jedi keep as close to using the Force for knowledge and defense as possible. The following films show even more murkiness in the Jedi's mandate, and their involvement in peace-keeping rapidly loses control. The Jedi do not seem comfortable with leading armies against armies. What do the Jedi do to pursue aligning their spirits with the Force, as a defense against killing for control instead of for peace? How do they find balance that keeps them from becoming Sith?

The attitudes of the Jedi in all the movies are the important links for us: they do not seek to obey the letter of the law; they seek to obey the spirit of the law. The result is that, amidst their preference for spiritual asceticism, the Jedi remain grounded. They know that they must stop an evil force in order for society to be healthy, even though they prefer meditation to fighting. This fighting for peace is, no doubt, a paradox that contrasts with the irony of the lack of peace they would experience if they did not fight. The Jedi are rooted in giving of themselves; their whole lives are dedicated to missions that help people free themselves. The Jedi do not store up earthly possessions or even collect wealth. Even their dress is simple. Contrast this to Amidala's clothing and her opulent world. For the Jedi, the quality of what goes on inside a person is more lasting and more important. All of these things qualify the Jedi to fight purely. They have nothing personal to gain from any fight. Even in the heat of battle between Qui-Gon and Darth Maul, Qui-Gon sits perfectly still and focuses his mind while waiting for an energy beam wall to retract. Obi-Wan has a more active way of focusing when, intent on the battle seconds away, a wall stops him from making contact. Neither Jedi wants to kill for killing's sake; they fight because the Sith are a clear obstacle to peace. The only peace the Siths desire is a destructive, controlling peace.

Ultimately the Jedi cannot be the peacemakers they seem without dealing with the sin, the wrong deeds and impulses, in their own lives. Call it being aware of their ability to use power for evil, and the natural inclinations we all have to take the easier, more seductive, path. Luke faces his temptations of anger, and we see Obi-Wan's temptation of looking primarily to the future, and we hear a little about Qui-Gon's history of bucking authority. It is important to being agents of peace to "take the plank out of our own eye" (Luke 6:41) before "taking the speck of sawdust" from the eye of our neighbor.

[74] THE QUALITIES OF THE FORCE IN LITTLE ANI (ANAKIN SKYWALKER).

Qui-Gon Jinn and Anakin's mother, Shmi Skywalker, discuss Anakin's uniqueness. Their dialogue goes back and forth. "He gives without thought for himself," says Qui-Gon. "He knows nothing of greed," she agrees. He has special powers. Qui-Gon informs her, "He sees things before they happen, which is why he appears to have such quick reflexes."

Anakin's character is first evidenced in his hospitality to get the visitors out of a coming sand storm. Once he discovers their plight, he immediately knows the only way to help them is to use his pod and pod-racing skills in the up-coming pod race to win enough money to buy the rocket parts they need. He willingly commits to a dangerous activity that could easily injure or kill him in order to help complete strangers. How often do we act like that? When we do act like that, we say, "But holy Lord, when did we ever invite you in before a sand storm, or volunteer our pod racer and ourselves to race it, and almost die racing, so that we could help you?" Then Jesus says, "Whatever you do to the least of these [people], you do it to me."

Anakin has no father; it is implied that he was immaculately conceived. Even his mother, Shmi "can't explain what happened." The theory emerges that since Anakin has such a high midiclorian count, perhaps he was conceived by the midiclorians, and as such is a convergence of the Force. So, the microscopic independent life forms that live in all cells as symbiants with them, who speak to us and tell us about the Force and the will of the Force, had somehow conspired to make Shmi pregnant. The *vergence* of Anakin causes Qui-Gon to think that he may be the fulfillment of a prophesy to bring balance to the Force. This is one more aspect in which we see Anakin as a Jesus figure.

What could the midiclorians be similar to in real life? A bunch of beings living in us could be like massive demon possession, Legion, or maybe this could be seen as the heavenly hosts or the Holy Spirit working in us. Both of these are far-fetched, and *Star Wars* is science fiction, not allegory, so pushing the connections in some instances can be a fruitless labor. Midiclorians are, however, extremely similar in word-sound and concept to mitochondria, the symbiotic organelles that convert and deliver energy and oxygen to our cells, and something we have read about in another children's science fiction classic, *A Wind in the Door*, by Madeleine L'Engle. Maybe midiclorians are like a spiritualized, sci-fi version of mitochondria. And perhaps midiclorians are encouraged by generations being faithful to God, and the blessings that come to "your children's children, to four generations." Mitochondria are inherited from your mother, in most cases, and so they are passed down the family line much like the blessings of a family that is faithful to God. Luke Skywalker did say, "The Force is strong with my family . . . ." And much of Anakin's inheritance came not only from the *vergence,* but also from Shmi, because even though she is not shown exactly as a Mary figure, she does exhibit high virtues just in the few minutes we are given to get to know her.

One last thought about the midiclorians: Qui-Gon tells Anakin that, "when you learn to quiet your mind, you will hear them speaking to you." When we are quiet and listen in our time of prayer, one thing we become aware of is that we must continually seek to not take for granted that this praying is to a real God. We are really, actually, in real life communicating with the holy God, the Creator of the universe and the King, Lord, president, prime minister of us all. It is not good to take this lightly, and for those who do not believe in God or in a God with whom we can know and communicate, this must sound very strange indeed. Actually, this whole book is quite silly if God is not real. One side note: It is important to be aware of the real Deity, and one way to keep aware of God is to learn the many names he goes by in the Bible. This helps to visualize the fullness of his identity. When we read Genesis, we have no definition of God, no description of his appearance. We continue to read, however, and hear about the things he does and what he says until we get a very clear idea of who is God, and what he is like.

Similarly, the main attraction in the character of Anakin is finding out what a special being he is because of what he does and what he says. Anakin, like God, is all about love.

[75] Qui-Gon gives Anakin some Jedi tips before the pod race.

Qui-Gon advises Anakin before the pod race to "concentrate on the moment" and to "feel, don't think." He also tells the boy to "use your instincts." And some people say that not much Jedi information comes out in these prequels! Sure, we have heard this kind of thing before; with three movies down we had better have heard about them! Still, it is nice to have a fresh take on these concepts.

When it is your turn at bat, you take all that you know about hitting a ball and hope that your body and mind retain the memory of all of the practice because at that moment you are no longer thinking, you are now acting. This is how it is with performance. Anakin is about to perform in the pod race; his goal, of course, is to be faster than anyone else. As with any goal we might undertake, the advice is the same: Learn. Study. Gain as many tools as are available to you first. Anakin had raced before, he knows about racing, and he is building his own pod racer . . . so he is fully familiar with the technical aspects of his specific racer and the strategic aspects of pod racing.

When it comes time to race, you take all these things and they become part of your subconscious. You act out of faith that it will all come together. In an event, knowledge becomes experience. In that moment, it is unwise to say to yourself, "Well, I learned this from this, so if I just . . ." Actions are much more immediate than that, and being in the middle of a race or a fight is not the time to begin to analyze. Instead, you do what Qui-Gon advises Anakin to do, to "concentrate on the moment." Do the very next thing that needs to be done, whatever that might be. This is where instinct comes in. You may have a lot of book smarts about racing, but good instincts are what proves your performance.

To some extent, faith is a performance. God assures us that we are saved for eternity, yet we have to "work out [our] salvation with fear and trembling." (Philippians 2:12) We accept God as real, Jesus as his Son, the holy Counselor's presence in our lives—and this is just the start of our training. Then we must work to know him better, to become stronger, just like a Jedi. Going through periods of intense training is good, and needed, but learning to be a Jedi is a lifelong process of practicing what you learn and believe. Having faith not only that God exists, but that he can be very involved in your life, is not just a matter of study. Having faith in God does involve study of the Bible's credibility and considering whether the philosophy behind it is credible. However, having faith is also facing the spirits of anti-Christ that teach a wrong or bad doctrine, as so many books and churches do today. Knowing what is good about them and what is not good about them is also important. It also entails observing the lives of the people who believe to see if they show something noteworthy, then finding out how to do these practices of faith such as praying, worshipping, and using the gifts properly so that we are more than simply another clanging cymbal. The performance of faith, then, is like letting go, like Luke Skywalker does while flying along in the trench of the Death Star. Whatever faith issue we face, we either exercise our faith and let go, or we fight to control everything. Anakin and Qui-Gon's approach to the race is like the life of faith, "Concentrate on the moment."

Flannery O'Connor expressed the mystery of writing, which is very much an exercise of faith, as a process in which 2 plus 2 never equals just 4. The mystery of the practice of faith is that you always get out much more than you ever put in. Faith is more than simple mathematics, and science is just a delving into the *how* and the *what* of our universe, not the *who* and the *why*. And you might as well forget about the *where*! Faith does not always make logical sense, and the more you expect something quantifiable out of it, the farther away you get. Shmi recognized Anakin's success in winning the pod race not in terms of the measurable—being faster than the other racers—but in terms of the deeper success. She said to him, "You have brought hope to those who have none."

Anakin was who Jesus would have been if Jesus were merely human. A great kid with quasi-supernatural powers and great gifts of selflessness and concentration, who eventually becomes disillusioned with the failure of the less-than-perfect people around him and becomes blind to his own failures, even to the point where he embraces evil and ends up as Darth Vader.

Qui-Gon shares with Anakin and Shmi that, "Our meeting was not a coincidence. Nothing happens by accident." Nothing happening by accident, though, would mean that the *Star Wars* universe is neatly and finely controlled. This hardly seems the case, given the haphazard nature of the Jedi adventures. Yet, there does seem to be a kind of order in the chaos of their experiences, so Qui-Gon is making quite a point in expressing that "Our meeting was not a coincidence." Indeed, their ship being disabled trying to escape from Naboo and only able to reach Tatooine, then stumbling upon Anakin who happens to be a *vergence* in the Force is clearly two things: a plot device and a working of the Force. The fact *Star Wars* begins with the droids also in the desert on this same remote planet (entry 2), and now this, creates the idea in our minds that the Force is present and active and blessing even the lowly Nazareth-like planet of Tatooine. It is also true that God does not always control everything precisely, as the Force does not in the *Star Wars* universe. God loves us enough to give the world its freedom, and within that freedom he is working, and then there are those things that are not his working. The way Qui-Gon rightly identifies their seemingly chance encounter as a moving of the Force is an excellent example, though, of the importance and wisdom in following God's guidance.

Once the Jedi Council determines that Anakin will not receive training as a Jedi, Qui-Gon tries to give Anakin at least the basic knowledge that will help him. On a docking platform just before they leave for Naboo, he tells Anakin that his focus will determine his reality. Just as in the death of Jesus, was Jesus simply being crucified unjustly or was he dying once so that we all might live forever if only we believe in him? If Jesus' focus was only the former, that his death was unjust instead of the latter, that this was the final work he was to do to forgive us, then he would undoubtedly have either hidden from the troops coming to get him or summoned thousands of angels. Instead, he walked towards them and said, "I am he."

Often there is purpose in the events of our lives that do not immediately seem apparent. If our focus is not to miss those hints, those clues, the coincidental guiding of the Holy Spirit, then our focus is to discover the purpose. This focus determines the reality of a life of purpose versus a meaningless life. If we believe only that life is meaningless, we will also interpret life around us as meaningless. Strangely enough, using this logic means that the same event might be interpreted by one person as clear evidence of the Force's moving while another person might see it as random meaninglessness. Therefore, it is how we choose to see events, and what we do because of those events, that determines whether we bring good or bad into the universe. It is amazing to see people from the same place in life go in completely different directions. Some people bring great things into the world, and others—whether they intend to or not—bring bad things. For example, take two classmates in school, each from the same level of privilege as the other, yet one ends up addicted to drugs while the work of the other brings love to millions.

One of the very positive characteristics of Generation X is that we have great powers of self-consciousness. Although this could stifle the working of the Force if we do not know when to let go, it is a given that we know a lot about ourselves in relation to our world. This is an issue that confounds most Baby Boomers. Yet, their great strength is our great weakness; which is doing something about an issue once it is known. If Baby Boomers sense the problem, and even if they only have the slightest clue of its answer, they rush to solve that problem. Generation X, though, sees through false answers easily, and knows the right solution to problems sometimes even before the problems are presented to them. What must baffle the Boomers is that we Gen-X-ers are often apathetic about going through with a solution. The truth that "Your focus determines your reality," says to Generation X-ers that if we do not fight our apathy and allow God to work through us toward the solutions that our lives need, then we will bring bad things into the world by default. In the example of Luke facing the Death Star in *Episode I: A New Hope*, Gen-X has issues with climbing into the cockpit of an X-wing starfighter. Once in, however, we excel at working with the Force. For Boomers, the hardest thing is to let go of the targeting system and trusting that the Force will move through to the solution. For Generation Y-ers, their hang-up is that they don't realize that the Death Star is evil. Gen-Y has all manner of abilities and skills, but grew up in a politically correct world where wrong and right are confused with each other and are sometimes said not to even exist. Gen-Y is not even sure it is OK to call the Death Star or the Empire as evil, because if it is, then so are we.

[76] THE CHURCH OF THE EMPIRE OF THE UNITED STATES?

The Jedi Council was unaware of the rise of the Sith even after a thousand years, and the Sith Lord was right in front of them, working with them the entire time. Mace Windu says, "Impossible," and "We would have known." Yoda responds, "Hard to see, the dark side is." Is it possible that the church in general, at least in the U.S., could be compared with the Jedi Council? Has the church become too comfortable and complacent, just like the government of the Republic? The U.S. is a big, shiny country. Have some of the guardians of our faith lost their way and the Force is no longer with them? Have we as a nation and a church been looking to externals too long? Has this caused us to smooth over and bury the real issues deep underneath the surface?

Are we forgetting to be calm, at peace, to sit and read the Bible, to meditate, to press into God for the answers, and to listen? Have we forgotten that living honestly and humbly often looks like living with a mess? It seems like many denominations get so caught up in being politically correct that they completely diminish the authority of the Bible. This is similar to the blindness of the Jedi Council to the evil right in front of them.

Have we exchanged a pursuit of Truth for a religion of *shoulds*, as the Jedi Council in *Episode I: The Phantom Menace* seemed to do? If the establishment of religion goes against the pursuit of truth, or the goal of knowing God better, the purpose of religion is lost. All the commonalities *Star Wars* has with Christianity, Buddhism, Taoism, etc., is good and affirming . . . but only to a point. It would be unsettling to think that this is all just the occupation of our imaginations. There must be something true and eternal to myth. Do we care if what we believe is just fiction or real? It is important to repeat that if Jesus was and is real, as in he was who he said he was, he has to be the most valid thing in everyone's life. The being that created all things coming down to a very special planet to be with creations he created very specifically to be in his image, would have to be the most relevant being to our lives, wouldn't he? If the historical

Jesus was not really God's son, then who cares—this is all a bunch of nothing.

Myth resonates truth to us, though, and we love *Star Wars* for it. If Jesus is real, he is the true myth (*God in the Dock*, C.S. Lewis) and *Star Wars* says a lot about his character. The real stickler is this, if the claims that Jesus made about himself are true, then no amount of saying, "You believe what you want and I'll believe what I want" is going to help any of us. We cannot make Jesus untrue for ourselves or anyone else simply by saying and thinking that he is not true.

What has all this to do with churches and empires? Who we are and what we say is true determines who leads us, and how he or she leads us. What is true—and our pursuit of that truth—is thus vitally important. If we forget to pursue truth as individuals, as churches, or as societies, then we will become like the Republic in *Star Wars* prequels.

[77] BUCKING THE SYSTEM, QUI-GON JINN STYLE. "THAT BOY WILL BECOME A JEDI. THAT I PROMISE YOU."

Qui-Gon Jinn brings Anakin back to Coruscant with him, taking him away from his mother in order to train him as a Jedi as the three of them agree. The Jedi Council is a little taken aback to learn that Qui-Gon was attacked during this escapade by someone—most likely a Sith—who is fully trained in the Jedi arts. The last known Sith disappeared more than a thousand years previously, the Council believes. In addition, the Jedi Council discovers that Qui-Gon has found a boy who he thinks is the fulfillment of an ancient prophesy. The Council's pride seems a bit hurt that it came neither upon the disease—the Sith—nor the cure—Anakin—on its own, but the Council members do their best given the circumstances. A decision is made that training Anakin to be a Jedi will not happen because the Council senses that the boy has too much anger in him. Qui-Gon rebels, saying to Obi-Wan, "That boy will become a Jedi. That I promise you."

He defies the opinion of the council, but respects their authority, after a fashion, and tells Anakin that since he is not allowed to train the boy, that Anakin should carefully observe all of Qui-Gon's actions. It might be that his defiance is due to his staunch belief that Anakin is the Chosen One, and as such will likely be trained in the future and thus the Council must, again in the future, change its mind because Anakin's destiny would by then be revealed. Anakin's bravery and heroics on Naboo and Qui-Gon's death reverses the decision, and Qui-Gon ends up being correct in his assessment.

In Qui-Gon's appeal to the council to take Anakin on as his Padawan learner, and consequently for Obi-Wan to take the trials and become a full Jedi Knight he mentioned that Obi-Wan had a lot to learn of the living Force, but that there was little else he, Qui-Gon, could teach him. This has a lot to do with his decision-making process, and why he is seen as always bucking the system. If a person is following God, it is possible that in one area he may seem liberal and in another he may seem conservative. Since God's Word is fixed and society is constantly in flux, the way we see things changes. Especially today, we say we believe in Jesus but it seems that many of us do not care too much to know him; we swing with the moral relativism of the day and try to interpret God through what we want him to be, not the other way around. Qui-Gon may very well think the Jedi Council to be morally relativistic because they believe the prophesy but refuse to accept Anakin as the fulfillment of prophesy when he faces them. The situation reminds us of John the Baptist preaching of the Messiah to come and the resistance of the established religion to accept Jesus once he became known.

Qui-Gon resists the shock and surprise of discovering both the Sith and the prophetic answer to the Sith in the same short visit to a remote planet and concentrates on what the living Force has to say about them both. But beware! This could only be true if the living Force is the same yesterday, today, and tomorrow. A dualistic view of the Force, which is how we are tempted to see the Force due to the few misleading lines previously discussed, would be changing all the time and lack continuity in its own self. If the Force were dualistic, Qui-Gon would be very turned around: one minute he would be filled with the light side of the Force and in the next the dark. Qui-Gon desires to "follow the will of the living Force." If he were subservient to a living, dualistic Force, he would always be in conflict between choosing the light or the dark. If the will of the Force turned dark, then he would have to refuse to mind the living Force. He would be set against it. As it is, even the midiclorians, who supposedly know the will of the Force and speak to the Jedi about it, have a will for good to happen. Qui-Gon is acting in the correct way, on the right path, because he follows a living Force that constantly works for good. In the same way water makes a strong bond with itself yet remains completely flexible and endures, so does the living Force, and so too is the living God who is in us and through us and all around us.

[78] A DISSENTING OPINION.

In the testing of Anakin by the Jedi council, Yoda and the council gang up on him in order to bring out the boy's main weakness. It is understandable that this harsh analysis must be given to a Jedi recruit, and especially one who has a midiclorian count higher than Yoda's *and* who is suspected to be the fulfillment of a prophesy *as well as* an immaculate gift from the midiclorians. It does not take the Council long to uncover Anakin's fear: fear of being away from his Mother and losing her, a very understandable fear. Yoda gives his big speech on progression of the dark side: "Fear leads to anger, anger leads to hate, hate leads to suffering."

Much earlier in this book, we discussed that there is a fear that is vital: fear of God and a healthy apprehension for bad things, especially the bad in ourselves. But Yoda goes further here to say that the end result of fear is suffering. Seems very Buddhist of him. What Yoda leaves out is that the lack of a healthy fear also leads to suffering. If you do not fear the effect of stepping in front of a moving bus and do so, take it on faith that you will be suffering, either from the pain of the collision or the sudden loss of the life you did not want to lose just yet. If you don't fear God and you die, take it on faith that you will be suffering.

[79] THE SAD END OF *EPISODE I*: *THE PHANTOM MENACE*.

At the end, Amidala does shed some of her naïve ways, and that at least is positive. She travels back to Naboo with the intent of suffering with her people. On the ride there, she realizes or rather is coaxed into seeing, the urgent need for an insurrection. Copying *Episode VI: Return of the Jedi*, the unknown power of a primitive people group—this time in the form of the Gungans—proves triumphant against the oh-so-powerful evil opposing team, this time in the form of the personality-less, over-powerful droid armies of the Trade Federation. The Naboo and the Gungan come together through the presence of the most unlikely of persons, Jar Jar Binks. The war is won accidentally in the most dire moment by Anakin's happy-go-lucky playing around in a Naboo star skiff . . . and the scene is no more serious than a roller-coaster ride. Qui-Gon is tragically killed and even more tragically ritually burned in front of the funeral party. Repetition can be a good and powerful tool that emphasizes the continuity of the world created by a set of stories. However, with *Episode I: The Phantom Menace*, we have an expensive imitation of the previous three films: Anakin blows the bad guy's space fortress and proves he is a special Jedi-to-be just like Luke Skywalker in *Episode IV: A New Hope*; the Gungans play the same role as the Ewoks; Qui-Gon dies for Obi-Wan as Obi-Wan dies for Luke; there is a ceremony at the end with the heroic group walking up steps to receive an award from Amidala just as Luke, Han, and Chewbacca do from Amidala's daughter, Princess Leia; and Qui-Gon burns on a pyre as does Anakin in *Episode VI: Return of the Jedi*. Time will tell if a younger generation likes this beginning of a prequel trilogy with the same devotion that *Episode IV: A New Hope* inspired in a generation growing up in the 70s and 80s.

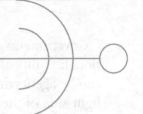

EPISODE II
ATTACK OF THE CLONES

[80] Behind the scenes.

There are so many visuals, so many different types of scenery in *Episode II: Attack of the Clones*. And there is so much activity and plot spinning that it is easy to miss out on what lies behind the scenes. This is purposeful. This is a busy universe—one like our own—filled with the beauty and over-activity that could lead us to be shrouded by an onset of evil, just as the Republic does in the form of the faithless and deceived Senators who ditch the democratic process for a much easier emergency powers act of governance that gives control to one person, the Supreme Chancellor Palpatine. The busy Jedi order, even the Jedi Council itself, has grown blind to the dark force that is growing unseen until it is suddenly dominant.

Aren't these patterns happening in our own world? George Lucas most likely intends these parallels, but this hardly makes them less true.

The satirical answer is that Americans love being busy so much that to say, "I am not busy," is almost worse for a reputation than admitting to being a terrorist.

The non-satirical answer is "yes, and . . . ." Yes, there are many likenesses of the Empire in our world; some of them in America, and some of them in many other countries in the world and the United Nations. When we are calm, at peace—not busy—we see something behind the scenes still further. This movie focuses on what happens when Anakin does not practice the Force. He strives, spins his wheels, and succumbs to temptation. The society around him seems to echo his decline. This pattern is true of us as well. Society can aid or suppress our tapping into the Force. Or said a different way, the way we are together as a community can bring health or injury to our individual practice of faith in God's presence and creative energy.

Governments, economies, laws, use of nature, priority of education, humility of a nation, and all the things that make up civilization can be agents drawing us individually and corporately closer to the light side of the Force. Unfortunately, the way we all get to a place where this is encouraged is not a very black and white issue. All the busy-ness of our personal lives, our careers, our entertainment, and all the domestic and international crises in our world today are just like Lucas depicts life in *Episode II: Attack of the Clones*. The best thing to do about all of it is this, once again: We must always find a place to be calm, to be still.

Be still and know that I am God. . . .

(Psalm 46:10)

Then we ask ourselves: how do we love God first with all that we are and how do we take care of our neighbors as ourselves? If we lose focus due to our busy-ness, we will unleash upon ourselves in a very real way the same kind of maelstrom the Republic releases upon itself.

Anakin is immature in his faith, and he tries to control the Force instead of letting it flow. Just like when we try to control the Holy Spirit, or when we try to control the Muse. Are they different? Commercial songs, paintings, stories, etc., tend to be particularly obvious examples. They are not from a person creating out of a love for truth and expressing it through a love for music, a love for images, or a love for stories and words. Commercial works are often simply the products of a company manufacturing these works out of desire for money.

This is why the fruit of the Spirit is called fruit. When we allow the Spirit to be in us, and we practice the spiritual disciplines, they grow out of us much like the flowing of the Force. How it happens is a mystery.

There may be a misconception that the flowing of the Force means that our work is effortless. The Jedi do not seem to win their battles effortlessly, nor do they gain maturity in the light side of the Force without expending much effort coupled with a purposeful decision not to use power irresponsibly, which leads to the dark side. The difference between struggling and striving in our work can be a subtle difference. The more we pursue truth, the more we use our abilities and our resources for others, the more we let go of self, and the more we acknowledge the living God, the more we understand the difference between struggling and striving. The dark side seems to have effortless power. Is this just a quality of being fully committed to self? If you do whatever you want as opposed to fighting your sinful nature when it crops up, you certainly have an easier pursuit of your goals.

[81] GREAT BAD GUYS.

It is worth repeating that *Star Wars* has great bad guys of all different shades? We are attracted to their marvelous powers and tangibly fear their incredible depths of wickedness. These figures don't secretly want to be good, or maybe came from a broken home and just need love (besides Anakin) . . . no way! They are pure evil, and nothing makes you want to have faith that a good higher power exists than the existence of a really, really malicious bad guy.

The seemingly benevolent Palpatine, subtly directing the conversation of Jedi Masters and Senators towards his own secret will, then turning around to direct his evil pawns as Darth Sidious (insidious); he knows no depth of evil. Before his disfigurement, he is handsome in his senatorial robes, then afterwards we see him shrouded with an awesome black-hooded cloak. As a politician, Obi-Wan notices that Palpatine, "is very clever at following the passions and prejudices of the senators." He orders the Jedi children slaughtered without blinking in *Episode III: Revenge of the Sith*, and he off-handedly orders the death of Queen Amidala and thousands of Naboo citizens in *Episode II: Attack of the Clones*. Lightning shoots out of his fingers . . . c'mon, that has to be the epitome of evil. What is most impressive about Palpatine is his worthiness. He is the slickest of politicians, has the keenest of minds, and is terribly organized to pull off this brilliantly strategic ascent to power, mostly in secret. As an adversary, he commands the utmost respect.

Count Dooku is also a great bad guy. The way he echoes Darth Vader of future episodes, "Join me," he entreats Obi-Wan, "and we will defeat Darth Sidious," is as ominous as it is welcoming. And why is it that all Sith pupils want to murder their masters? It seems like an accepted practice. Of course, Dooku never mentions to Obi-Wan that he is also Darth Tyranus, Sidious' new Sith pupil, and the one who hires Jango Fett to be the clone donor, or that he has fallen for the dark side of the Force because it makes him so much more powerful that he, too, can shoot lightning out of his fingers and make large objects hurtle towards his opponents. If Obi-Wan had known that Dooku was Darth Tyranus, Obi-Wan would have quickly identified the Sith Lord as Palpatine. The great evil thing about Dooku is that he was once a Jedi Knight, so he knows all the Jedi ways and weaknesses. However, as the name of his base planet Geonosis implies (think Gnostic), Dooku leaves the Jedi order for an extreme version of mysticism that is no longer grounded in truth. So he is this alternative good guy, potentially a very cool quirky character, but his Gnosticism is the agent of seduction that leads him into darkness instead of to a higher light, ironically forsaking that for which he originally had been searching. Besides, Dooku is so old, how could we possibly think he is much of an adversary in a fight? Sure he has menacing garb and demeanor, but his age leads Obi-Wan and Anakin to underestimate him in the final fight. Only Yoda proves to be his match.

Darth Maul is the quiet type. His face is almost clown-like, but his flexibility, martial arts and two-sided lightstaff are ominous enough. A lot of the Jedi-Sith fighting includes words as part of the fight, but not with Darth Maul. He is all business. There is no chivalrous banter with him. He would just as soon slice you open as look at you.

Finally, it is particularly excruciating to watch Anakin's slow decline, and this twists our sympathy for him. We want his mother freed way back in *Episode I: The Phantom Menace* when we first met her. We want Anakin and Amidala to be together, even though this leads him down the path of deception and forbidden relationships as part of the Jedi order. Anakin is quite purposefully the James Dean-like rebel of *Star Wars*, increasingly the cool adolescent set against the cause of the adult Jedi. He wants power for himself and is not afraid to express it. He does not often bow to those he is supposed to serve. He wants to see himself as equal to them; as a teenager he is typically afraid that he is not their equal . . . he is not at all comfortable with the Jedi submitting themselves to service and rebels against being seen as anyone's servant. He continually thinks of himself and the Jedi as superior, which is at once true and then untrue in the very stating of it. How creepy is it when Palpatine says to Anakin, "Trust your feelings, then you will be invincible." Palpatine feeds his ego and says that Anakin will be the most powerful Jedi ever. You can just feel him slowly corrupting and muddying Anakin's thoughts.

It is sad and true that the rise of a dark lord is exciting to watch. The flourish of the Jedi is so mundane because they do not seek glory for themselves. For Anakin to come along, then, and be so skilled that his fame has spread in the *Star Wars* universe, already *Episodes II* and *III* is something we want to watch, in spite of as well as because of the horrible path he chooses. We are dying to see how it happens. It is more than just good, old-fashioned suspense. Humanity has never stopped creating idols, and Anakin "James Dean" Skywalker embodies that sad but true mythical weakness in all of us: we are fascinated with heroics and want to see the glory of a talented individual, even if the glory itself leads him to evil.

[82] THE WAY A JEDI DISAGREES.
ANAKIN IN FRONT OF THE JEDI COUNCIL.

In the Jedi Council chambers, the way a Jedi who is in the center of the Council circle, giving information and receiving instruction, presents his disagreement is by stating the obverse of whatever is said. The Council and the disagreeing Jedi both actively pursue understanding the truth of that opposite. Both sides give the benefit of the doubt to the other, and emotions are taken out of the dialogue as much as possible. For example, the Council tells Anakin to take Queen Amidala home. He replies that it will be difficult to convince her to go because she is the resistance leader, the one who is most active in resisting the military creation act. The Council come back with guidance for Anakin to speak with the Supreme Chancellor and to request his help with this matter. The communication is successful between them, and both appear to feel heard, understood, and their efforts are unified. The communication is successful. However, it might also be pointed out that this scene is an example of how the Force is not with the Jedi: they are unable to discover or realize that Palpatine wants to create a clone army and that Amidala's departure—since she is leading the charge against creation of just such an army—will very much play right into Palpatine's plans.

[83] THE WAY A JEDI LOVES.
ANAKIN AND AMIDALA POSE AS REFUGEES.

Scene: Anakin and Amidala, on their way back to Naboo, are posing as simple refugees. On the transport, Amidala asked Anakin about life as a Jedi.

Amidala – "It must be difficult having sworn your life to the Jedi . . . not being able to visit the places you like . . . or do the things you like . . . ."

Anakin – "Or be with the people I love."

Amidala – "Are you allowed to love? I thought it was forbidden for a Jedi."

Anakin – "Attachment is forbidden. Possession is forbidden. Compassion, which I would define as unconditional love, is central to a Jedi's life, so you might say we're encouraged to love."

Episode II: Attack of the Clones

Attachment is forbidden. It is not clear what this means because the Jedi certainly are attached to the light side of the Force. They are attached to their training, their masters, and their way of life. Based on the context, the attachment of a sexual relationship is forbidden.

Possession, the love of material things, is also forbidden. We can be thankful to *Star Wars* for promoting the idea that it actually is a good thing not to accumulate material wealth.

Compassion is central to a Jedi's life. The young Padawan was to err with regards to defining compassion only in terms of unconditional love. Compassion certainly involves quite a bit of unconditional love, but that isn't the only component. It is also true that this kind of love is central to a Jedi's life, as we know it. The Jedi dedicate their lives to loving others. This part of their mission is very merciful.

Out of the four classic Greek loves that C.S. Lewis writes about in *The Four Loves: Affection, Eros, Charity, Friendship*, only Eros is forbidden to a Jedi. To their fellow Jedi and to those around them, the Jedi practice affection, charity, and friendship . . . so what is so particular about Eros that it would be forbidden to the Jedi? The Jedi, much as the monks of various religious orders in our world, probably discovered that sexual relationships are so powerful that they interfere with a person's life-long commitment to a religious order. This is a logical understanding. Even the apostle Paul advised that life is more singly focused on God if you are not married and do not have a family. Our completely sex-driven culture does not often present the option of just being single, non-sexual, and cool. How obtuse! We can be thankful to *Star Wars* also for at least these images of what this might look like, even though the discussion occurs in the middle of Anakin's pushing forward his attraction to Padmé.

[84] To the center of gravity's pull.

Scene: Obi-Wan Kenobi traces down the origin of a poison dart that kills the assassin who almost kills Padmé/Amidala. He visits Yoda, who is training Jedi younglings.

Obi-Wan — "This is where it ought to be . . . but it isn't. Gravity is pulling all the stars in this area inward to this spot. There should be a star here . . . but there isn't."

Yoda — "Most interesting. Gravity's silhouette remains, but the star and all its planets have disappeared. How can this be? Now, younglings, in your mind, what is the first thing you see? An answer? A thought? Anyone?"

Jack, a Jedi Child–"Master. Because someone erased it from the archive memory."

They step away, then Yoda continues.

Yoda — "Truly wonderful, the mind of a child is. The Padawan is right. Go to the center of the gravity's pull, and find your planet you will."

Episode II: Attack of the Clo

Obi-Wan, of course, does travel to this part of the galaxy, and he does go to the center of gravity's pull and finds the missing planet, where he also discovers a clone army being created, along with the bounty hunter he seeks.

This imagery has another metaphor, apart from the plot. We do not empirically know that God exists. We will always need to have faith. Even for the Israelites who saw Moses after he talked to God, and for whom God miraculously provided food, water, and a pillar of flame or cloud to follow in the desert, and who gave them impossible military victories, needed to have faith. Even the apostles who saw Jesus walk on water, perform hundreds of miracles, come back alive after being crucified, and lifted into heaven on a cloud needed to have faith. For us, having faith in God is like having faith that a star system exists though we do not see it on our charts. We can see gravity's pull towards God in our scientific questions of how did the universe come to be created, and in our theological questions of: if God is; and if so, then who is he; and what is he like. All of life pulls inward to the Creator whom we cannot see, and yet towards whom we continually gravitate even in our not seeing. Life cannot be created out of nothing, and yet God must have done so. We know that nothing cannot create something. A Creator God who creates marvels out of nothing must be the center of the pull of this gravity.

[85] Jango Fett, just a man in the world.

"I'm just a simple man trying to make his way in the universe," Jango Fett tells Obi-Wan on Kamino.

This is self delusion and ignorance at its finest. Jango must continue to lie to himself in order to believe that his actions are just those of "a simple man, trying to make his way in the universe." The idea of living a simple life and just doing your thing, as this statement implies, is a fine one. This philosophy could show a complete disregard for living in community, and in Jango Fett's case, it certainly does. Not that a person must live with others and be some happy little Smurf, but a person committed to this point of view might have little regard for how others live or even care whether his living adversely effects them. Jango cares only for himself. Even his son, Boba, is a clone of himself. He is similar to Lando and Han in their self-centeredness; the difference being that they are under no illusions in their earlier lives—they are all about themselves and readily admit it.

I once had a friend who believed this way. He pursued a mutual friend's wife, they had an affair that he based on their common connection of childhood abuse, and asked her to leave her husband. He also thought of himself as just a simple man in the world. In order to get what he wanted, however, he convinced himself that this husband, one of his best friends, was not worthy of his wife; that a relationship with her was worth more than a friendship with him; and most importantly, that his desires were more important than anything or anyone. His greed back-fired on him, however, and instead of getting what and who he wanted, his attempt at "trying to make his way in the universe" destroyed his friendships with those who cared most about him.

On the corporate level, companies that help governments suppress individual freedoms are another fine example of this type of thinking. They are "just companies trying to make their way in the universe." Their lack of responsibility not only hurts and kills innocent lives, but damages their own lives and souls as well.

[86] ANAKIN AND SHMI SKYWALKER.

Anakin's attachment to his mother leads to suffering. Again, this plot line in the movie originates from a Buddhist concept that attachment leads to the karma of suffering. It is not logical to assume, however, that this concept dictates Anakin should not love his mother, or long to be reunited with her. Perhaps it could be best understood as "inappropriate attachment leads to useless suffering." Certainly Anakin's suffering, in the form of his nightmares and predominant thoughts of his mother, is the Force pulling him to rescue her. He searches out his mother because he feels her pain and wants to save her from it. The anger that eventually comes out of Anakin, fed partly by missing his mother and partly by blaming himself for her death, is borne out of stifling any attachment to his mother, not the attachment itself. It is the Jedi Council's fault and Obi-Wan's fault for not listening to Anakin, not heeding his dreams, and not understanding that this attachment to his mother is a good and healthy thing. It would be better if Obi-Wan or the Council had freed her, or at least allowed Anakin to visit her during the ten years of his training. Not allowing this created a vacuum of desire for his mother.

What happens instead? Anakin and Amidala fly to Tatooine to find her. Anakin discovers the source of his bad dreams—their timing has coincided exactly with Shmi's abduction by Tusken raiders. Back on Coruscant, Anakin was feeling the echoes of her pain. He journeys out alone on the chopper in search of her. He finds her, but she lives only long enough to see him, tell him she loves him, and dies in his arms. In his anger, he slaughters the entire encampment of Tusken men, women, and children.

Afterwards, back at the moisture farm, he and Amidala have an important conversation brought about by his mother's death.

Amidala – "I brought you something. Are you hungry?"

Anakin – "The shifter broke. Life seems so much simpler when you're fixing things. I'm good at fixing things . . . always was. But I couldn't . . . ."

(stops working, tears in his eyes)

Anakin — "Why did she have to die? Why couldn't I save her? I know I could have!"

Amidala — "Sometimes there are things no one can fix. You're not all-powerful, Ani."

Anakin — "I should be! Someday I will be . . . I will be the most powerful Jedi ever! I promise you, I will even learn to stop people from dying."

Amidala — "Anakin . . . ."

Anakin — "It's all Obi-Wan's fault. He's jealous! He knows I'm already more powerful than he is. He's holding me back!"

Amidala — "Ani, what's wrong?"

Anakin — "I . . . I killed them. I killed them all. They're dead, every single one of them . . . not just the men, but the women and the children, too. They're like animals, and I slaughtered them like animals . . . I hate them!"

Amidala — "To be angry is to be human."

Anakin — "No, I'm a Jedi. I know I'm better than this."

Episode II: Attack of the Clones

In the development of Darth Vader, this conversation is pivotal. Anakin has committed a huge crime. He slaughters innocent life because of his anger. He becomes more powerful, but also slides farther down to the dark side. He cannot forgive himself and he does not confess to his master, that we know. If he is not held accountable, either by himself or by others, forgiveness is hard, if not impossible, to achieve. He resigns himself to what he starts to see as his fate.

Also in this conversation, Anakin expresses his lust for power like never before. He wants to be the fulfillment of the image with which Palpatine has been stroking him: the idea that he can become the most powerful Jedi ever. Anakin even wants to stop death. He hates his flaws, and hates his humanity. He starts to think of death and imperfect life as something to fix and control.

Finally, at Shmi's funeral, Lars shows thankfulness for her life, and thankfulness that she was part of his life. Anakin can only think of himself. He is obsessed with his failure and, in this time of letting go, he grabs a handful of sand by which to remember her.

[87] Jedi Blindness.
"It is time to inform the Senate that our ability to use the Force has diminished."

In *Episode II: Attack of the Clones*, many of the Jedi are either blinded or discover they have been blind. Most notably in the Jedi Council, this happens to Yoda and Mace Windu.

Yoda   –   "Blind we are if creation of this army we could not see."

Windu   –   "It is time to inform the senate our ability to use the Force has diminished."

Yoda   –   "Only the Dark Lord of the Sith knows our weakness. If informed the senate is, multiply our adversaries will."

Episode II: Attack of the Clones

For ten years they have not sensed the creation of a clone army, or even perceived of its making in any of their Jedi disciplines. For years before that, they did not realize a dark Sith Lord was not only plotting, training an apprentice, becoming stronger, but doing so right under their noses.

In our world, we can perceive and intuit dark things, dark people, dark events, and know where these lead. Jesus says that living in the world where many people hate Jesus and his followers makes us like sheep among wolves. As a result, Jesus says in Matthew 10:16 that we are to be as shrewd as snakes and as innocent as doves. We are to know, therefore, that evil is the way things tend to go, and we would be wise to be observant of these tendencies.

In the busy activities of the Jedi, Yoda and Mace Windu and likely the whole council let down their guard. There had been no Sith for a thousand years, after all. Mace and Yoda certainly saw the creation of a clone army without their knowledge or foresight as a weakness not easily corrected. Liken this to our not testing the spirits, so to speak, or to not questioning our spiritual leaders, making sure their advice is sound. In America, at least, if not in other countries, parishioners today are like the Jedi who have not seen the darkness growing even in their own churches. Now the darkness is very powerful.

This whole movie is full of Anakin not being observant of the living Force and practicing what he has learned. Another example happens in the fields of Naboo when he and Amidala are picnicking and flirting. Anakin states that politicians should be made to agree. The idea is very tempting, especially in a heated or lengthy debate. Amidala challenges that this sounds like a dictatorship, to which Anakin responded, "Well, if it works." Amidala stares at him in disbelief, then she lets the topic slide, along with many of her other reservations about Anakin's character. The fact that she does not address the issues makes her culpable, too; she is once again an ignorant part of the decline of the Republic. It is amazing how our blindness, purposeful or not, can open the door to bad things.

Obi-Wan's blindness comes in the form of not practicing being calm and at peace. In his failure to fully connect with the Force, Obi-Wan allows himself to be overloaded with activities. He does not perceive that he is "being overly critical" of his Padawan as Anakin complains to Amidala. He does not address Anakin's dreams or treat them as valid. Thus, he neither senses Anakin's pain nor brings to the Council what he knows of Anakin's attraction to Amidala. These mistakes, born out of busy-ness, turn out to be fatal to the Jedi order.

On a grand scale, the Jedi world is just as blind in its arrogance and supremacy. Even the librarian tells Obi-Wan, "If a system does not appear in our records, it does not exist." Sometimes when an organization gets too big or too comfortable, it loses sight of what is possible and dwells only on the probable. When this happens, we lose our concept of mystery being real. This is one sign of a culture in decline.

Yoda understands this at the end of *Episode II: Attack of the Clones*. He perceives that the Clone Wars have only just begun, and that the clone army that saves them signifies the beginning of the end of the Republic.

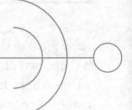

REVENGE OF THE SITH

[88] IRON SHARPENS IRON.

As iron sharpens iron, so one man sharpens another.

(Proverbs 27:17)

We have better things to sharpen iron with today, but we do not have anything better to sharpen mankind with than ourselves. Often we lose this wisdom and either try to replace mentoring and friendship, speed it up, or get rid of it. So'it is invigorating to see the mentoring and the apprenticeship in *Star Wars*. Even though Obi-Wan is now a master on the Jedi Council and Anakin a full Jedi, there is still learning and teaching back and forth between them. The Padawan learner that studied for years with the master has not only learned the trade of being a Jedi, but is known by the master as a person of value. Meanwhile, the learner also comes to know his teacher as a master in full context of foibles, personal hang-ups, as well as his individual strengths in the Force. These relationships foster not only better, more complete, teaching, but also encourage the value and identity of an individual as a person. The Jedi are more fully known than—in our world, for example—working at a company a few years then moving on.

Personal responsibility is established and expected in the Jedi system of training. It is difficult to do this today. Mentorship is often limited by the time and authority given to it, hence the knowledge that a master and an apprentice share of each other is limited. With only minimal time together, the best side of each is undoubtedly what the other will see. Diminishing a master's authority over an apprentice means the learner no longer must submit to the same extent. It is difficult for growth to occur in a master/apprentice relationship under those conditions. True growth lies in long periods of time spent watching the behavior of a learner and correcting him or her. There is also a burden on the master to continually improve himself and be worthy of training an apprentice. Even Qui-Gon Gin and Obi-Wan Kenobi, excellent teachers though they are, have problems that get in the way of perfect training.

There is also an adversarial nature to the sharpening. Obi-Wan, in *Episode I*, was learning from Qui-Gon, and part of this learning was testing himself against Qui-Gon in what he said and thought. In this process Obi-Wan begins to see how he is different, has different skills than Qui-Gon. Then, as a master himself, he trains Anakin, teaching him all he knows, and Anakin bucks his authority, to a certain extent, in the search for who he is in the Force.

It is good for men to get in touch with their feminine side, and this is happening more and more frequently. The Jedi's sharpening of each other, however, encourages us to move towards a time when both women and men can learn about masculinity.

This is not the soft, accepting feminine thing. This is testing, trying, challenging each other. This is learning from the competition we love so much in sports, and bringing it rightly into all the world. Backstabbing, tricking, deceiving, pulling a fast one—anything unfair is weak and shameful. There is honor in a fair fight. We need to learn how to compete and do battle, to do it well, and with style. Reintroducing masculinity into our touchy-feely society looks a lot like telling someone they are wrong, and then proving it. It looks like the restoration of reason to our thought process, and a willingness to be proven wrong. When it comes time to fight, myth is a good encourager—it helps us understand that when a conflict is a good one, it is good to have a taste for battle. What battles stimulate your taste buds? Do you want to fight the rampant heresy in the church today? Or the greed of some of those in government? Or the human rights violations of massive corporations? The Jedi way is to learn both sides so well that you can argue the opposite of your belief. This is the training. Fighting in the issues of today, with masculinity like a Jedi, is to be a rational, reasonable person. This means that you concede a point when there is truth in it, and acknowledge that you are fighting for something greater than yourself and not for your own glory.

When the Jedi and the Sith fight openly, there is an honesty that comes out. In our world, people fighting for good often appear wrong and people fighting for the wrong thing are not entirely bad; in fact they usually start from a nugget of truth to get to their error. In *Episode III: Revenge of the Sith*, when Anakin and Obi-Wan fight Count Dooku, each person is seen honestly and plainly. In those moments, they are the fullest and most open about who they are as possible. There as no holding back, no clogged pores, so to speak: you bring the fullness of yourself to meet the fullness of the other. This is also iron sharpening iron.

There is no sharpening when you try to deceive the other. Anakin killing Dooku would have been right and respectable to both of them. But the insidious Palpatine makes evil of it by convincing Anakin that it is done out of revenge. Dooku is a Sith, they are fighting each other to the death, so there is honor and respect in that death. Anakin believes Palpatine's twist on it, and this serves to draw him one step closer to the dark side.

[89] ANAKIN'S DREAMS, AGAIN,
AND A FLAWED VIEW OF DEATH.

Anakin has dreams of Padmé dying in childbirth. It is hard for us to know if the dreams we have mean what they seem. It is a good impulse that Anakin wants to protect her. It is his fear of this happening, however, that forces the dream into literal reality. He joins the dark side to save her, and it is his joining the dark side that kills her. Because she cannot follow him down the path he is traveling, she tells him so at the end, she no longer wills to live. Would she have died if Anakin had not joined the dark side?

Anakin seeks out Yoda to discuss this premonition, without giving him the specifics that would expel him from the Jedi order. Yoda advised him that a fear of loss is a path to the dark side. Simply having a fear of loss is natural, though. The answer is balance: it is not good to let any fear paralyze you. Anakin responds like a Sith, "I won't let this come true." Yoda then launches into a flawed view of death.

He says, "Death is a natural part of life." True enough, death is a part of our physical bodies. "Rejoice with those that transform into the Force. Mourn them do not. Miss them do not," Yoda continues. Even if you think that life transforms into pure energy, it is just unhealthy in this universe or the *Star Wars* universe not to mourn the dead, and not to miss the dead.

What does this phrase, "transform into the Force," mean? Supposedly Jedi, Sith, and everyone who dies become particles of light, part of a mystic whole, increasing the energy of the Force. Obi-Wan and Yoda and Qui-Gon before them find ways to collect their particles and materialize after their physical death. A Christian way to see this, though this was surely not the intended meaning, is that God made us as individuals, and the Bible supports the view that we stay that way after we die. Our identity remains, though we will join together with angels and archangels and all the heavenly host in praising God. This involves becoming part of one energy, which is remotely similar to the idea of transforming into the Force. In this way, we can find common ground with Buddhism, Transcendentalism, and Mormonism, which one finds more similarity with these ideas in *Star Wars*. Where Christianity separates from these is in believing that God creates us as separate individuals, and that our sin is further proof that we are not one with him.

Then Yoda instructs Anakin that attachment leads to jealousy, and that this is the shadow of greed. Anakin asks what he must do, and Yoda tells him to, "let go of that which you fear to lose." This mental picture really rings true. It is like the story of the rich young ruler. He fears losing his wealth, and knowing this, Jesus tells him to let go of his wealth if he wants eternal life. The rich young ruler goes away sad, presumably because he knows that he cannot let that part of his life go. Anakin holding on is like the image of the clenched fist of the rich young ruler versus the open palm. If you, the reader, are not sure whether you are like this, not sure if you clench your fist in fear of losing something, the answer is simple . . . you do. We all do at times. Try giving away possessions, particularly if you are in the western world. Imagine in your mind figuratively holding that which you fear to lose. It could be material possessions, children, wife, parents, siblings, friends, food, anything. Now imagine letting go of them. In your mind, and in your body, clench and unclench your fists. This does not mean you love them less than is good and right; it means you do not love them too much or too little, not inappropriately one way or the other. It means that you love them with freedom and do not expect any love back. It means that you let go of controlling or neglecting, and you allow yourself to relate to God straight up, not bent by any other thing or person. We cling to people and things out of love for what they mean to us, not out of love for those people and things by themselves. Anakin was not holding on too tightly to the idea of Padmé for her sake. The over-love was not directed at her, but rather it was all about Anakin's feelings of possessing her. This letting go is not an easy thing to do, and it is not supposed to be something you only do alone. We are meant to have each other to help us do this, and even then, God really has to assist us through our unnatural clinging.

[90] Use your feelings, Anakin. In the Jedi Temple, upon appointment to the Jedi Council, and at home with Padmé.

If Luke Skywalker used his feelings too much, Anakin uses them too little. Obi-Wan urges him to use his feelings in his relationship with Palpatine. He begs Anakin to look at the obvious, that there must be something behind Palpatine's unprecedented placement of Anakin on the Jedi Council, and that it is more than suspicious that he has stayed in office much longer than the normal length of his term. Obi-Wan wants Anakin to intuit that something does not seem right. Anakin does not heed Obi-Wan's advise.

Anakin fails to use his feelings in other instances as well. He fails to feel the rightness of Yoda's advice and the twisted nature of the Chancellor's counsel. He fails to use his feelings and all of his other Jedi and human faculties to realize that killing Jedi younglings is wrong, and that Padmé and Obi-Wan speak truth to him. His desires blind him to the truth. How often do we let our desires blind us from the truth?

He comes close to seeing the truth in a conversation with Padmé.

Padmé   –   "I wonder what is happening to the order. Sometimes I think this war is destroying the principles of the Republic."

Anakin has the answers within his grasp. If he had followed his feelings and devoted himself to finding the answer, he would have stuck with the Jedi order, killed Palpatine, become a Master-Jedi, and Padmé would not have died. He would have received all that he wanted if he had placed the plight of others and the pursuit of truth ahead of his own desires.

Padmé chimes in, agreeing with him, potentially bringing him closer to the truth, but he interprets her words as those of a separatist.

Padmé – "What if the democracy we thought we were serving no longer exists? And the Republic has become
the very evil we've been fighting to destroy? This war
represents a failure to listen."

Episode III: Revenge of the Sith

If we feel or if we think that the country in which we are citizens is
in a war that represents a failure to listen, what do we do?

[91] PALPATINE MAKES HIS MOVE
TO RECRUIT ANAKIN. PART ONE.

Episode III: Revenge of the Sith is the darkest film in the six-movie *Star Wars* series by necessity of its place in the story line. This was where Anakin's loyalties divide and where he questions what he thinks he knows. It is an ambiguous time for him; relationships and world views are not clear to him. He is in a fog; he even tells Padmé that he feels lost. The audience is not lost, however. The movie is not filmed through Anakin's point of view, so we do not wonder which is the correct path that he must go down. The makers of the movie most clearly and directly show us how Anakin is traveling down a wrong path. We see and we agonize over his wrong choices. In spite of, or perhaps because of, the darkness in *Episode III: Revenge of the Sith*, the *Star Wars* universe is elucidated as a moral one more than it ever had been. When Palpatine calls for Anakin in the theater under the guise of informing him that General Grievous and the separatists have been discovered, then has him sit down and starts his direct recruitment, we have no misconceptions about the malevolence of Palpatine's intentions.

First, he commences with the stroking of Anakin's ego. "I would worry if they didn't pick you . . . ." and later, ". . . you are by far the best choice . . ." Palpatine says. Anakin is thinking how high an opinion Palpatine has of him. Then Palpatine moves on, playing to Anakin's sympathies, which he just bought with the previous compliments. "The Jedi are planning to betray me," Palpatine warns conspiratorially. Palpatine, however, does not stop there. He drives the wedge in a bit further. "They (the Jedi Council) don't trust me, the Senate, or democracy for that matter." These statements are pretty risky, because they are very bold statements that Anakin would see right through were he not too busy thinking of himself. Anakin's reaction to these statements tell Palpatine exactly where the young man's allegiance stands. "Remember your first teachings: All who gain power are afraid to lose it," Anakin says to his new master. Imagine if Anakin responds with, "Including you?" the Chancellor might well have backed away from him, realizing that Anakin thinks for himself and does not just automatically believe whatever the most powerful man in the galaxy tells him is truth.

Anakin half-heartedly reacts in defense of the Jedi, "The Jedi use their power for good," he tells Palpatine. The Chancellor's response continues to belittle the Jedi with half-truths that play into Anakin's suspicions and weaknesses. "Good is a point of view, Anakin." Here is why the yin-yang symbol, which very much represents a Jedi philosophy, cannot represent the relationship between good and evil, and cannot represent one power. First, because the Chancellor uses this statement to deceive Anakin. If good was a point of view only, then Palpatine would not have been deceiving Anakin, even though we are undoubtedly led to believe he is. Palpatine would just have been showing Anakin a larger world, another option. Second, if the term *good* is meant in the over-arching, absolute truth definition, as in good versus evil, as here it is, *good* is not a point of view. It exists whether or not Anakin sees it as such. *Good* continues to be *good* even after Anakin switches over to the dark side. If *good* were a point of view, then whatever we think would be *good* because we are *good* and we are thinking it. I know some Christians who have that kind of skewed thinking. The worst part of it is, if you really think this is so, it is likely that just as Anakin is completely blind to this fact you are as well!

Palpatine continues, "Sith and Jedi are similar in almost every way, including their quest for greater power." To say the Jedi seek greater power is a loaded statement, of which the nugget of truth is that yes, they do. The fuller picture is that the Jedi seek to be greater by being lesser. To this statement, Anakin tries to give a proper defense, "The Sith rely on their passion for their strength. They think inwards, only about themselves," Anakin says to Palpatine.

"And the Jedi don't?" comes the Chancellor's rapid rebuttal.

"The Jedi are selfless," Anakin contends. "They only care about others." With this statement, Anakin unknowingly is successful in stopping this line of further deception by Palpatine. However, both men know that Anakin is at least one Jedi who is not completely selfless.

Palpatine either has great intelligence or surveillance technology, or he can read Anakin's thoughts and dreams. Perhaps Palpatine plants the dream of Amidala dying in Anakin's mind, because he then launches into a play for Anakin that strikes at his most vulnerable spot . . . Padmé. Supposedly, no one knows about their marriage, their pregnancy, and certainly no one else knows anything about Anakin's nightmare where he sees her dying while in childbirth. Anakin makes no connection, however. He thinks it merely a coincidence that Palpatine starts telling him the tragedy of Darth Plagius the Wise—someone who can use the dark side of the Force to influence the midiclorians to create life and also keep people from dying. Anakin must think that since he was created by a convergence of the midiclorians, this story must apply to him, and that perhaps the dark side was the stimulus of his creation . . . so the dark side can't be that bad. That, and a promise that knowledge exists that can save lives, convinces Anakin that he must know more about it.

The more skilled or talented we are, the more of a person we are, the more likely it is that both good and evil will vie for our attentions. Anakin is supposed to be the Chosen One, conceived by the midiclorians, the one who brings balance to the Force according to prophesy. No doubt he is considered a superstar in the Jedi world, and as he progresses, he only confirms the thinking of many Jedi that Anakin is indeed the Chosen One. If we know that the good side has already made a play for us, then mathematically speaking, the evil play is yet to come. Anakin could have traced back to when he did not feel confused, when he last felt clarity in his life, and could have deduced exactly where evil starts misting in, trying to mix with the good, thus confusing him. Thinking of how we could do this in our own lives is difficult. We tend to be so future focused, or so busy, that taking time in quietness to try to remember back to events is difficult to even imagine. However, God can reveal this kind of thing to us in prayer if we ask and listen.

Palpatine finishes the conversation, knowing Anakin has taken the bait and is now interested in knowing how to prevent death. He knows also that Anakin will not question the source of this line of thinking. Anakin is most willing to be deceived. "The dark side is the path to many abilities some consider to be unnatural," Palpatine concludes. This is a true statement, and one of the dark side's most pernicious attractions for many of us.

"What happened to him?" Anakin asks. The Chancellor reels Anakin further in with the story of Darth Plagius growing so powerful that his only fear is the loss of power. He teaches his apprentice everything, Palpatine tells Anakin, and the apprentice of Darth Plagius the Wise kills his master while he sleeps. Palpatine feels the tension of Anakin on the hook and lets Anakin run with the line. "Is it possible to learn this power?" Anakin asks innocently.

"Not from a Jedi," is Palpatine's reply. Not much needs explanation here except that our point of view in this movie helps us understand better than Anakin what is really happening. In our own lives, we do not have the benefit of a third-person point of view. Therefore, it is possible for us to follow in Anakin's footsteps and start believing a heresy or a cult if we fail to question ourselves, refuse to maintain a balance of mind and heart, or ignore the prophets around us.

[92] Palpatine makes his move to recruit Anakin. Part Two.

Anakin reports to the Council that the location of General Grievous is known. However, Obi-Wan is chosen by the Jedi Council and sent with troops to kill Grievous and end the war. The Council sends Anakin back to obtain Palpatine's reaction so the Council will know whether Palpatine will end the war as he has promised. This also implies Palpatine's stepping down from power.

Once again, Anakin steps off the path of feeling the Force as the Chancellor begins stroking Anakin's ego. Let this be a lesson to us all. Like Romans 12:3, ". . . Do not think of yourself more highly than you ought . . . ."

"The Council does not trust you. Why did they not make you a master?" Palpatine asks Anakin. With an increasing sense of entitlement, Anakin admits that he does feel excluded by the Jedi Council and that he knows there were things about the Force that its members are not telling him. OK, if anyone says to you, "They know your power will be too much for them to control," or anything of the like, please assume that—as talented as you may be—whoever said this is trying to give you a big head, and there is most likely a motive behind their statement. If you are grounded in understanding your sin, you can move forward. If you actually believe that you are as great as that flattery, then you will lose sight of this important truth about yourself.

Palpatine entreats Anakin to see through the fog of lies that he claims the Jedi have created, and wouldn't you know it, Palpatine himself offers to help Anakin know the subtleties of the Force.

Now that he has tagged the Jedi with causing all of the confusion that Anakin feels, Palpatine pushes Anakin to make a decision. Thus, Palpatine emerges from the very fog that he creates and offers to make everything clear for Anakin. "How do you know the Force?" Anakin asks, thinking that he is only talking with a powerful and experienced politician.

"My mentor taught me," Palpatine replies, also mentioning that his mentor taught him much more about the nature of the dark side.

Palpatine – "If one is to understand the Great Mystery, one must study all its aspects, not just the dogmatic narrow view of the Jedi. If you are to become a wise leader, you must embrace a larger view of the Force."

Episode III: Revenge of the Sith

Do you see the dualism acting like a higher wisdom rather than discerning what is good? This sounds like the serpent in the Garden of Eden, or if Anakin bears any similarity to Jesus, then this is the temptation of Satan, who offers the world to him. Anakin takes what is offered, however, and Jesus did not.

To those who think that the Force is dualistic: Why is the dualism here portrayed as evil? To those who think the Force contains both good and evil, but is not dualistic: Why is Palpatine's view evil?

The Chancellor impresses Anakin even more with the knowledge of Anakin's secret marriage and pregnancy. The dark side must be powerful if he knows about us, Anakin must be thinking. Palpatine here is selling Anakin on a life of significance, of conscience. Who among us would not desire those things?

Anakin is left with a choice. The Dark Lord suddenly reveals himself and is supposedly vulnerable, and yet the Dark Lord claims to possess the ability to save Anakin's wife and child. Yet it is Anakin who is fully vulnerable emotionally and spiritually to the evil Darth Sidious, who even exploits Anakin's anger towards Palpatine for being the Sith Lord by enjoying the focus and strength of Anakin's reaction—as if Anakin were already using the dark side of the Force.

Palpatine encourages Skywalker to go back and discover the Jedi Council's intentions. Here, he presents Anakin with a "who do you like better" scenario. As long as the real issue of "you must make your own decision," is not addressed to the confused Anakin, the Chancellor has more than a fighting chance of landing him as his new apprentice.

Mace Windu leads a group of Jedi Knights to confront the Sith Lord, and all are quickly killed except for Windu. Windu and Palpatine—now revealed as the Sith Lord Darth Sidious—duel, and of course, Anakin—our boy wonder—comes racing back to catch

Windu about to kill Palpatine, which Anakin claims is not the Jedi way.

"He must stand trial," Anakin contends.

The Chancellor is on the windowsill and acts as if he is too weak to fight. Mace Windu declares that Darth Sidious is too dangerous to be left alive, moves to strike him down, and Anakin lops off Mace Windu's arm. No sooner does he do this than the not-so-weak-after-all Palpatine proclaims the power of the dark side to Anakin by showing him unlimited power as he first electrocutes and then effortlessly tosses Mace Windu out the open window.

Palpatine fools both Mace Windu and Anakin Skywalker. It likely would have taken both Jedi to strike Darth Sidious down, and this is yet another opportunity where Anakin can fulfill his destiny. More importantly, Anakin is worn down in the process of going against what his conscience is screaming out to him to do. He is left exhausted and confused, his only thoughts are of himself, and what he believes is good for him. In this way, Anakin is like Adam and Eve, wanting a power that evil had promised them, a power they were deceived into thinking existed simply for the taking.

[93] WHAT HAVE I DONE?

As soon as Darth Sidious/Chancellor Palpatine utterly destroys Mace Windu, Anakin Skywalker is struck with the reality of his situation. The impact of it all, that he assists the evil Sith Lord in destroying a leader of the Jedi Council, whether this is done purposefully, causes Anakin to despair. "What have I done?" he cries. And from then on he is resigned to what seems his certain destiny. How could he now go back? The goodness inside him is so oppressed, and his desire to save Padmé so strong, that he succumbs to the evil lord completely. "I will do whatever you ask. Just help me save Padmé's life. I can't live without her," Anakin tells Darth Sidious, who immediately nets his catch by telling Anakin they must now work together to discover the secret of stopping death.

Even in his depression and with all the evil bearing down on him, Anakin must surely have thought, "But you led me to believe you already knew how!" Outwardly, however, he kneels and submits completely. "I pledge myself to your teachings," Anakin says to the Sith Lord.

From this point on, the only commands from Darth Sidious to Anakin are to go and kill people in order to become more powerful, and Padmé dies before Anakin/Darth Vader can help her. In short, the new Darth Vader might never have received anymore teachings.

There were other times in his progression towards Darth Vader when Anakin wondered the same thing again, "What have I done?" Before and after he kills the Jedi younglings, he seems to ask himself this, although this may simply be my interpretation of the way in which Hayden Christensen acts out his part. Again, he asks the same question immediately after he murders Nute Gunray and the other Trade Federation leaders. We see Anakin/Darth Vader standing on a balcony before Padmé arrives in her silver ship as tears run down his face. He understands in that moment that evil power is eating his soul. This lays the groundwork for Luke, who feels the good remaining in Vader. The very issue of his regret and embarrassment for choosing evil is working at him all the way back in time to the present movie, where he has just become Darth Vader. He is angry with himself for committing these acts and for following the Emperor-apparent, and his anger at himself lashes out to everyone else, even as he tries to find a likely person to blame. His killings become a way to appease his own anger. He cannot forgive himself. He does not believe that he should be forgiven. He is too proud to confess. He acts with wild abandon, hoping to die. He becomes a breeding ground for hate. In short, his situation is the perfect combination for creating a Sith.

Vader must soon come to see what we have already glimpsed in Palpatine from the start: Palpatine knows he was evil and knows he fights against truth; he has not deceived himself. But if he can deceive others into believing that he is not evil—that he does, in fact, love truth—then Palpatine can take those people down with him, like Lucifer, and that is his goal.

[94] In touch with the cosmos
and, at the same time, in touch with reality.
A difficult thing to do, this is.

Even as Yoda commands armies of Wookiees, he feels pain inside himself when Anakin moves to the dark side. Then again, Yoda feels this disturbance of the Force and almost doubles over in pain when the Jedi start to be slaughtered following Palpatine's issuance of Order 66. This is the same sensation that Obi-Wan feels when Alderaan is blown-up by the first Death Star.

Yoda is simultaneously in touch with what is happening in the battle as well as the cosmic pulse of the Force with these deaths happening far away from Yoda's location. Yet, Yoda is able to live in the present, to be mindful of the Force, and to be mindful of the treacherous thoughts and sounds directly behind him. When Order 66 comes to the clones on this planet, they march up behind Yoda. He senses their thoughts and hears the sound of their weapons preparing to fire. He quickly slices off both of their heads in one stroke. Yoda then has to escape. How is it that Yoda has a secret shuttle hidden in the bushes? We are left to wonder whether he suspects this action by Palpatine, or if he leaves it there in case the droid army wins, or whether perhaps he did it as the practice of a good warrior. Whatever the case, Yoda is the epitome of awareness that use of Force can bring to us. Although Yoda and the rest of the Jedi are in a defensive posture in relationship with the dark side, and have no idea how to handle the mess in which they find themselves, Yoda continues to use the Force and to practice his own teachings as best he can in the midst of colossal failure. He does not get caught up in the details of war to the extent that he is unaware of the Force—the spiritual climate of the universe. Does Yoda intentionally walk with a cane in order to slow himself down and stay in touch with the Force? If Yoda lived in our world, he would be fully living in the presence of the Holy Spirit.

[95] VADER'S FIRST AND LAST LIES TO AMIDALA.

Anakin/Vader returns home to Padmé immediately after killing Jedi children and lies to her. She saw smoke pouring out of the Jedi Temple across the city, and feared that he also may have died. One can make a case that, at least spiritually, Anakin does die at the Jedi Temple, and physically lives on only as Darth Vader.

Anakin tells Padmé that there was a Jedi rebellion to take over the Republic. As proof, he tells her that he witnessed Master Windu's attempt to assassinate Chancellor Palpatine. Sure he did, but Padmé would have had a completely different opinion of this event had Anakin told her the rest of the story. Thus the half-truths of the Sith begin in Anakin. She asks what he is going to do. Again, he lies by saying that his loyalties are with the Chancellor, with the Senate, and with her. What's worse, he tells her that many Jedi have been killed, not bothering to mention, however, that he is the one who led in their slaughter.

This interchange ends with Anakin informing Padmé that the Chancellor has given him a special mission to go and fight separatists in the Mustafa star system and thus end the war.

The last time the lovers see each other is when Padmé is told by Obi-Wan that Anakin has turned to evil. She does not believe him, however, and travels to Mustafa to confirm for herself whether this is true. When Anakin starts talking to her on Mustafa, however, Amidala knows he is going the wrong way.

"I am more powerful than the Chancellor. I can overthrow him. And together you and I can rule the galaxy, make things the way we want them to be," he tells Padmé.

The more Anakin tries to do things under his own power, the more disillusioned his reality becomes. Contrast this with Jesus saying to Paul, "My grace is sufficient for you, for my power is made perfect in weakness" (2 Corinthians 12:9). And then in the apostle Paul's teaching, "For it is by grace you have been saved, through faith—and this not from yourselves, it is the gift of God—not by works, so that no one can boast" (Ephesians 2:8–9). Anakin's sin comes not from any inability to follow through on his statements, instead it arises from his attempt to take God's place; he boasts of his works. What drives him insane is that he fails to acknowledge his humanity. A universal truth of our humanity is that for all of our strength we are still weak . . . and to not admit this is to refuse God's grace. The Jedi are strong when they allow the grace of the living Force to flow through them, so that they are instruments of good, and not the good itself. Anakin tries to be the good itself, to be the Force.

[96] ABSOLUTES VERSUS EXTREMES.

Note: In case you are reading this entry in random order, entry 38 also deals with extremes versus absolutes. Also, the usage of the word *extreme* in this entry does not pertain to extreme sports.

In the last battle of the movie between Obi-Wan and Anakin, Anakin is so far gone to the dark side and insanity that he shouts the lunacy that he has brought peace, freedom, justice, and security to the new Empire. An important step in becoming the very thing you swear to destroy is denying reality. You must force yourself not to care about what is real or what is true . . . you must instead try for the exact opposite. "If you are not with me, you are my enemy," Vader says to Obi-Wan's reasoning.

He understands now that Anakin will not turn back from the dark side, and that you do not try to dialogue with darkness. So Obi-Wan responds, "Only a Sith deals in absolutes. I will do what I must."

It is an important distinction that a Sith deals in extremes, not absolutes. An extreme is about ultimatums such as the one Anakin gives Obi-Wan. An absolute is about the freedom that balance brings. Anakin has come fully into that which he began innocently on Naboo with Padmé, saying that senators—and, by extension, everyone else—must be made to agree. His extreme measures to force into existence peace, freedom, justice, and security instead bring about controlled order at any cost. He ends up with the opposite; war not peace, oppression not freedom, injustice not justice, and insecurity instead of security. Like love, he cannot coerce these ideals into being.

Conversely, Obi-Wan practices absolute love, which requires the balance of wisdom. He loves the Force and once loved Anakin. Obi-Wan understands that to kill Anakin with a lightsabor is far better than to allow him to be enveloped by hate. This love is in line with the light side of the Force, which is why Obi-Wan says that he will do what he must.

Another difference between extremes and absolutes is that an extreme leads to hate, an absolute leads to love. The battle ends with

Vader saying, "I hate you." To this, Obi-Wan responds, "You were my brother. I loved you."

This scene takes place on the red and black molten world of Mustafa, and this whole world, down to the river of fire, is purposely hellish. It echoes images of Satan battling God when the angel Lucifer tries to copy God's creative nature of love. In his inability, his striving, did he create extremes as a cheap imitation of absolutes? You can imagine God saying, "You were my most beautiful creation. I loved you." Lucifer might have spit back, "I hate you," out of envy for wanting to be the Creator. Then God casts Lucifer out of heaven. If God did this to the angel of light, and you and I are not angels of light, then what must his absolute love look like when exercised upon us?

[97] THE PHILOSOPHY OF MAGNETISM?

At the end of *Episode III: Revenge of the Sith*, Yoda and Darth Sidious fight. The closer they get to each other, the more their respective powers repel the other away, much like trying to join similar poles on two magnets. The same thing happens between Obi-Wan and Vader in their concurrent battle. Both pairs are evenly matched as the highest and second highest of their respective orders.

In the match-ups between Yoda and Darth Sidious, Obi-Wan and Darth Vader, it is their personal accomplishments as individuals that causes the equivalency of this magnetism, so to speak. It is a testament to the easy and quick power that the dark side brings that Vader and Sidious almost defeat Obi-Wan and Yoda. Of course, Anakin is already powerful in his own right before he becomes evil, but he lacks the judgment and wisdom that time, meditation, and experience bring. The blessing of his outstanding abilities is also a curse in that their development outpaces his emotional and spiritual growth. Becoming evil purified his purpose—maturity is not needed to be evil—and this allowed dark power to flow quickly through him and level the playing field against Obi-Wan. In similar fashion, Palpatine/Sidious does not have the eight hundred-plus years of experience that Yoda has with the Force, yet the dark side allows Sidious to come close to besting Yoda, and at least shocks him into accepting exile on Dagobah.

So we ask the same thing Luke asks Yoda on Dagobah, "Is the dark side stronger?" Yoda adamantly tells Luke no, that it is easier and more seductive, but in this scene it sure seems as if the dark side is able to compete, if not win. Despite the quasi-stalemate between Yoda and Palpatine, Yoda does go into exile, after all, and Obi-Wan does fail to finish the job and kill the young Darth Vader. What comes after this movie is a nineteen-year reign of evil and terror, culminating in the events that precipitate *Episode IV: A New Hope*. So how can the dark side not be seen to be at least as powerful as the Force? More importantly, if this myth is to resemble reality in any fashion, what hope do we have against evil forces? Must we be eternally stuck in the sway of power between good and evil as they repel each other and vie for power as these forces alternately take supremacy over the other only until they are forced back into subjugation? This is the sickening spin of the traditional view of the yin-yang symbol/Emblem of Chi.

If we believe that this *Weltanschauung* is all there is, then I would have to answer yes. The fight taking place at this intersection is not only the symbolic and actual culmination of the Republic's decline, it is the crux of a six-film series. It is also an excellent operatic ending to a powerful film trilogy, and provides the climax for a classic film. However, it also begs the question whether this yin-yang transition between good and evil is inevitable. In a yin-yang sense, it would appear so. The preeminence of good is followed by the dominance of evil and vice versa; on and ever on in a never-ending circle. From a factual point of view, however, Lucas and company have shown multiple reasons for the decline. The Jedi do not stick to their training, they are not still and quiet, and they do not listen to the Force. The Republic did not believe in its own ability to face the separatists, but rather panicked and gave emergency powers to Supreme Chancellor Palpatine. Does this sound familiar to anything happening today? Ironically, neither the Republic nor the Empire ever address the problems that the separatists are supposedly having with the status quo. This questioning alone would likely have revealed the conspiracy behind it. So the decline of the Republic was not inevitable, it was avoidable. There were many signs and warnings along the way that, if heeded, could have prevented the rise of the Emperor and his evil Empire. There is nothing in this trilogy or the next that indicates the case is hopeless or inevitable, or even just the way of things. Ultimately, the magnetic repulsion between good and evil characters is based on skill and situation, and not a comment on the larger powers of good and evil outside of those characters. All the rushing around and busy-ness of this prequel trilogy lends power to the evil side and diminishes the power of good. This is the lesson we are to take from this parallelism.

In our world, there seems to be this same magnet attraction and repulsion between good and evil. Evil seems to crop up where we least expect it, especially in relation to ourselves. It can be hard to believe that the work of Jesus on the cross was the final victory, though not chronologically, and that evil/death/Satan has already lost.

[HIDDEN BONUS ENTRY]
WHO PLAYS JESUS IN *STAR WARS*?

Although this whole book is dedicated to those places in *Star Wars* where Jesus shows up figuratively, philosophically, and in all other wise, this entry is devoted to Luke and Anakin, whose characters most evidence the person of Jesus, and who can be seen as the most obvious direct metaphors for him.

In the original trilogy, Luke Skywalker is the most likely Jesus figure. Besides being the main character, he is the human who performs miracles and points to wondrous signs, so to speak, by his use of the Force. These works he accomplishes through the teaching of Ben Kenobi—Holy Spirit—and Yoda—Father. Luke is the hero, and just like Jesus, he sacrifices himself for his friends. If numbers are your thing, Luke actually sacrifices himself for his friends three times, one major time in each movie: 1.) When he attacks the Death Star in *Episode IV: A New Hope*, 2.) When he goes to Bespin in *Episode V: The Empire Strikes Back*; and 3.) When he surrenders to Darth Vader in *Episode VI: Return of the Jedi*. In *Episode V: The Empire Strikes Back*, he loses his right hand, and this can be taken as symbolic of Jesus sitting at the right hand of God, the Father, only Luke Skywalker is obviously a much more flawed creature, and pretty whiny at that in the beginning. Luke's artificial right hand would then be a sign that he is like Jesus, but does not achieve exact likeness. Was Luke killed and resurrected like the Christ? No, but his flying into the trench of the Death Star, letting go, and falling down the shaft of Bespin and his being led into the Emperor's Chambers on Death Star II are all powerful images of Luke descending into darkness and then emerging victoriously into the light, which one might argue is very savior-like. However, Luke is never persecuted by the masses, forced to endure torture, and neither presents himself nor is he presented by the filmmaker as a substitute Jesus. He does represent a return to the universe of the Jedi, however, and in this way, Luke fulfills a gospel-like role to teach and spread knowledge about the Force. The gospel of Luke Skywalker is that of learning to use a supernatural power that is available to all, much like the gospel of Christ, and although we never hear Luke learn that love is the key, it certainly seems to be. Luke's actions also follow through with this love. Luke is much more the hero archetype than the savior archetype, though of course the above examples are in the paths of both archetypes.

In the prequel trilogy, Anakin bears an even closer resemblance to Jesus. There is the natural selflessness that he and Luke initially have in common. They both use their power to help others. The most scandalous Christ-like feature of Anakin is that he has no earthly father, but is born of the midiclorians and Shmi Skywalker. Because of this, Anakin is also seen as the fulfillment of an ancient prophesy, just as Jesus was prophesied to be the Messiah. Anakin is, perhaps, the most naturally-gifted Jedi ever; his use of the Force seems at times almost to be anointed. He is very much a messiah-like figure. Most unfortunately, in *Episode III: Revenge of the Sith*, Anakin comes to see himself as the savior of his people, and in this he becomes the anti-Christ figure, going against the prophesy that he would "bring balance to the Force." Instead of developing into a more selfless person, he becomes full of himself.

[98] How to avoid Anakin's fate.
A practical application of Jedi principles.

Part 1

The Bible passage from John 15 has been mentioned a few times already, but there is something extra in that chapter that fits the ending of this book. A prophesy exists that Anakin will bring balance to the Force, which he does finally accomplish in *Episode VI: Return of the Jedi*, the chronological end of this movie series thus far. In the Bible, John 15:7 and 8 provides a great clue as to how to avoid the same sort of downfall that plagues Anakin. As a reminder, this is where Jesus talks about the vine, and how the vine gets pruned of those branches that are not producing fruit. Jesus tells us how not to get pruned at the outset.

> "If you remain in me, and my words remain in you, ask whatever you wish and it will be given you."

Then, in verse 8,

> "This is to my Father's glory, that you bear much fruit, showing yourselves to be my disciples."

The hard part of faith is the first part, "remain in me." As soon as we ask what we wish, the question of whether we have remained in him becomes very apparent by the things for which we ask. Anakin does not remain in the light side and this becomes readily apparent when he "asked what he wished," which was for more power for himself, originally intending to conquer death and evil. He never arrives at the point of understanding that fulfilling the prophesy is not within his power; only with the living light side of the Force in him can this be done. Anakin is strong, young, able, and famous. All of these things cause him to think highly of himself even as they hinder his knowing the light side of the Force and the true love behind it. The closest thing we have to a Jedi in real life probably looks like the weak or the childlike because it is easier for one of them to understand a need to remain in God.

Part 2

Here is a rather practical application of Jedi principles, and it serves me well. When I desire something, I am learning not to embrace that thing too quickly, but rather hold the idea of it gently in my mind and simply think about my need of it. In this way, there is no need to rush to judgment whether it is all good or all bad. I think this is part of the balanced life of a Jedi. I mostly practice this with possessions and jobs. I recently almost bought a house, and it did not work out. My feelings were not overwhelmingly sad or overwhelmingly happy. I do think it is important to feel, and not shut one's self off from feelings, but the whole "trust your feelings" and "feel the Force" thing is really only half the story. I think a Jedi actually uses his mind, and consciously practices the non-possessing of things, even in the imagination. I was not too unhappy that the house deal fell through because my wife and I asked the seller to knock off a certain amount of the price, based on how much we knew the immediate repairs might cost. We even paid specialists to help us find out those costs. We based our offer on what we could afford. In our own minds, we gave the owners freedom to make their own decision about our offer. They had the freedom to accept or reject our offer regardless of how we felt about it, of course, but letting go of what we felt they should decide really freed us up as well. I would not have been overly happy about buying the house if the deal had gone through, either, because I knew about the money and effort that it would require to fix. I say I did not feel too happy or too sad, but I did have happy and sad feelings, I just did not let either get out of hand. We prayed and trusted God to help us make our decision. How can we know whether we had faith in this instance? How do we know we made a right decision? There was no writing on the wall explaining exactly what to do . . . so we don't know anything with certainty. But, this is what faith is all about.

The experience just seemed like a Jedi thing that my wife and I were able to hold the idea of the house in our mind and not get too attached. Make no mistake about it, we were consciously thinking about the Jedi and the Force during this decision, and those images helped us. We planned, held the idea of the house a little away from ourselves in our minds, we did not cling to it or depend on it or consider it a part of ourselves, and I think we learned an important Jedi lesson.

Part 3

A little journaling: So I need to practice this Jedi way of being. I am very tempted to be angry at someone who my wife and I feel is treating us poorly. We have to coordinate efforts to a small capacity with this person, and I really want to do anything that will disrupt her demands, her work, her success, just because she is being rude to us. This sounds vindictive to me, and I am fairly certain she treats many people like this, and my showing up where she is going to be would be a disruption she deserves.

In my attempts to practice what I am writing about, I am trying to breathe first, and remain calm and at peace before I make a decision. Immediately, my mind goes to what I will not be doing by showing up when this person wants me not to show up. I will not be writing this book, and that is important to me. I will be spending my energy to effect negativity on someone, and I am concerned that this gets me in a negative groove. Yet, my flawed mind still is working behind the scenes to finagle a valid reason to show up. I definitely do not feel like I am smoothly gliding along, a sensation I get only when the Force is definitely with me. I feel stunted in my thinking, and I am not thinking as much. I do feel a small amount of rage, and it is difficult to let go of this person's doing us wrong, and what justice should mean for her.

I think most pop-psychology would say that I can get through this and do the right thing on my own, and they are partly right, of course. No other person is going to drag me up the hill to interrupt her but me, and no one is going to keep me down here working but me. Still, I can find no reason to try to do this alone if I believe that God is with me to some extent and will help, especially if I ask. So I have been praying that God will forgive me for feeling ill-will towards this person, and asking for peace, and it comes into my head that even if this lady does something else against me or my wife, or something I might perceive as such, it is OK to allow that to happen. In that sense, I welcome the opportunity to show her love by forgiving her and I do not want to return bad for bad. God must help me do this as it is not a natural action for my flawed mind and heart.

I am feeling more calm now. In the middle of my chest there is more breathing room than before, it was getting a little tight. I think I am ready to go back to work. Pushing forward and writing can be a difficult enough process. Even following this distraction in my head causes me to feel like a trashy person, and it takes a while to refocus. I will not allow it to govern me. In my imagination, however, I am twirling the lightsaber and getting into attack position.

P.S. The end of this little story is that I was able to concentrate on working, I did get the vengeance thing out of my head. Unbeknownst to me at the time, my wife had a good conversation with the lady around the same time that I was working through this issue . . . and though my wife was able to be nice, I think she was unconsciously an obstacle to this person's plans.

P.P.S. To tell you the truth, postures of the Jedi getting into their ready position is something I imagine in my head a lot. When I am faced with temptations, I imagine wielding a lightsaber and facing the temptation in Jedi combat, and I imagine slicing right through the impersonation of my temptation. I have found this very effective. Also, I have noticed that Luke and Obi-Wan often hold their lightsaber at the ready or whatever it is called—around the middle. I heard a homily recently about the stomach being the center of joy, and the priest said that he imagined this is a posture of giving and receiving from the soul. Hmm, I wonder if there is a connection?

Part 4

The dark side is like living a lie. Even one small lie can be uncovered, and when it is, we have to face it or cover it with another lie. Sometimes our very movements, the way we move around town, can be dictated by a lie. If a person is having an affair, for example,

I do not think they could freely move through the streets without deceiving everyone that they are not living a lie. The more openly they come and go, the more brazen a follower of the dark side they become. The purer we are, the more we have confessed our sin, given it up, and received forgiveness, the easier it is to walk any-where—we have nothing to hide, nothing that will find us out. More importantly, even when living with a small lie, we still must deceive others. We have started down the path to the dark side, even if in only one part of our life. We know this is true because when we try to imagine coming clean, we realize that we have to go back to admitting we did something wrong, and then also we must admit that we tried to cover up that wrongdoing. Dark and light are two different paths leading to two different destinations, and when we remember a lie in our own lives, I think we understand this. The power sources are very different. It does not matter if you are Joe Christian, Joe Buddhist, or Joe atheist; we all know at least a little about lies, and we know how they drag us down.

[99] THE SPIRITUAL DISCIPLINES OF THE FORCE.

There are actual spiritual disciplines that exist in our real world. If you are bored or listless or curious, then these are for you. You will uncover in learning about these disciplines a depth that you hardly thought imaginable in this life. Honestly, if you are Hindu or Muslim, or even a Christian for that matter, are you going to go anywhere near a Bible, much less acknowledge anything is true in it? Well, in the same way you acknowledge truth in *Star Wars*, why wouldn't you?

This entry is not to teach about the spiritual disciplines. This entry is to compare them to the Force.

Prayer is like reaching out with your feelings. Prayer is like listening to the midiclorians. Prayer is what happens when you are calm, at peace. Prayer is like connecting to the living Force, feeling it flow through you. It comes to this: do you want to talk to the Creator or not? This discipline is odd in that it is perfect in the first moments you ever do it yet it takes a lifetime to perfect the art and attitude of prayer.

Bible reading, analyzing and memorizing are analogous to Jedi training. Here is where you learn the character of God through the words of God. "I have hidden your word in my heart that I might not sin against you" (Psalm 119:11). When shiny things—words, ideas, people, etc.—tempt you away from the light side of the Force, God's words to you in the Bible help you stay centered and focused. How do you know what is true versus what is not? How do you recognize a cult? You start here, with God's revelation of himself to us. This must be similar to how the Jedi learns of the Force in the first place.

Worship: Suffice it to say that Yoda is right, we are luminous beings. We need worship to recharge our luminosity and to express that light in voice, the position of our bodies, and in the position of our spirits. Think of worship as having the same benefits as exercise has for skin; sweating unclogs the pores and helps the skin to breathe just as worship unclogs the pores of our spirit and helps it to breathe.

Meditation: We get the idea Luke is meditating as part of his training on Dagobah, and we see Yoda on a kind of meditation cushion in *Episode III: Revenge of the Sith*. This is the practice of getting a clear signal, so to speak; it is hearing what God is trying to say to you so that you can do it. Yoda says, "You must clear your mind," and this means you must empty your mind of all the garbage, which to my experience is best done by confession and maybe even counseling, then filling it with God's known words to us from the Bible. What happens when Luke has the right frame of mind? Success, as in *Episode VI; Return of the Jedi*. What happens when Anakin does not have the right frame of mind? Insanity and failure, as happens to Anakin in *Episode III: Revenge of the Sith*.

Life-style is a discipline. Most of you reading this book, myself very much included, have way more than you need to live, and you indulge ourselves with pleasures great and small. Consider every bit of extra in your life, which is most of our life-style, something we are held accountable for using resources rightly or wrongly when we face judgment. This applies even to our entertainment. Slow down in the enjoyment of what you imbibe, avoid excess, live simply, and remember that there is no try, give until it hurts, do not accumulate treasures on earth. What does this mean for each of us? Each person must determine this individually, but it could be very exciting, mysterious even, how the extra can be used for the welfare of others. One of the biggest extras many of us have is information. Giving of information to help our neighbor is a good way to live, even though this sharing takes building friendships and relationships. The Jedi lived very, very simply in an age of plenty.

Along with this is a commitment to service. This is one external that distinguishes a Jedi from a Sith. Do your religious or political leaders serve themselves? One of the great problems in this world is that authority figures serve themselves. Some governments serve themselves by showing preference for a friend's company in giving out contracts. Others take outright bribes and kill for power. Many religious leaders exalt themselves. Part of a Jedi's life-style is service because this is evidence of selflessness. There is something about self that tends to lead us astray. For this reason, the way we live, the way a Jedi lives, is to be seen as a discipline.

If you are interested in plumbing the depths of who you are spiritually, and if you want to relate to your Creator more fully, *Celebration of Discipline* by Richard Foster is the classic portal. The book is like marijuana; an entry drug that leads you to other drugs. In his book, Foster includes disciplines that *Star Wars* does not really touch on like fasting, confession and solitude.

[100] EVIL IS BEAUTIFUL.

One thing *Star Wars* could have addressed to a greater extent: be wary of things that look beautiful and filled with light. At least, we do see both Padmé and Anakin tricked by the seemingly wise and benevolent Palpatine. Evil often appears to be very good. So many *Star Wars* fans revel in the excitement of Darth-mania because the bad guys are so vivid and interesting, and this is fine, to a point. Even Hayden Christensen, who is Anakin/Vader in the prequels, is beautiful on the outside. Beside this, however, the dark side is not presented as particularly alluring except to those like Anakin who are deceived.

In real life, however, there is so much that either is evil or leads to evil that also appears very attractive that it is hard not to fall for it. If something, someone, or some idea seems like a good idea—seems beautiful—then we tend to accept it.

To this end, here are a couple things in *Star Wars* that are not very helpful and potentially dangerous to the eternity of your soul if accepted as real: The idea of power, light, energy, the Force without the one-true God to create it is at the top of the list. It is a very nice idea to just have an energy that we are part of, and that we can learn to tap into. However, as explained earlier, if followed to its natural conclusion, this is a very detrimental line of thought. The idea is very seductive, however. The second beautiful yet dangerous thing is not being in touch with our sin. Clinging to the light side of the Force, willing ourselves to be a good person, is admirable but faulty if there is no understanding of those things we do and be that go against what God tells us is healthy for us to do and be. Sin is like a huge splinter in our skin; if we do not remove it, it will fester. This is not an issue I see addressed very well in the *Star Wars* movies. The beautifully evil nature of this is that sin not existing is a great idea. Finally, it is very possible to worship the Force, and in so doing we misplace the purpose of the Force in the way that the Force is written about in this book. 1 Corinthians 13, the love chapter of the Bible, sets us straight in this regard. The supernatural gifts that the Holy Spirit gives us are great, and they are similar to the power of the Force in many metaphorical respects. Using the Force, using these gifts, are pointless and annoying if they are not used for the purpose of love. The purpose of the Force in our world—the reason it exists and is good to learn about and use—is love.

[101] AGE OF REASON + AGE OF MYTH = GOLDEN AGE?

In the book version of *The Power of Myth*, journalist author Bill Moyers interviews Joseph Campbell, the preeminent scholar on myth. They discuss violence in the Middle East as it was going on around the time of the interview, 1985 to 1986. Moyers asks what Campbell thinks of the violence, and Campbell replies,

> "It says to me that they don't know how to apply their religious ideas to contemporary life, and to human beings rather than just to their own community. It is a terrible example of the failure of religion to meet the modern world."[10]

When Moyers asks Campbell what new kind of myth is needed in the world today—for religious groups to understand each other and not kill each other—Campbell replies that we need myths that identify with the whole planet, and that the original thirteen colony/ states of the U.S. represents a good model of coming together out of mutual interest, "without disregarding the individual interests of any one of them."[11] Campbell goes on to point out that the United States was able to do this because it was the first nation built on reason, and he used the mythic symbols on a dollar bill to demonstrate the founding father's commitment to these ideals. America's founding fathers believed in reason rather than the European power structures they escaped from, he said, and that reason is more like God—the eye of the pyramid—on the dollar. He says we have gotten away from this, and perhaps he is right. A return to classical education, where reason and logic are taught and emphasized, sounds so good as to almost be obvious. When religion is mentioned, many of us go mushy in the head. Yet, it seems fairly obvious that any country that governs itself with reason is a wise country. A revitalization of these basics in the United States is vital to the ideological storm that is brewing. If children, and adults, can be taught that reason can be applied to all aspects of our way of life, including religion, it would be much less likely that such a rational person would become a terrorist.

Still, Campbell never gave a very satisfactory explanation of what myth has to do with reason. Certainly, he thought the formation of the U.S. on reason—as opposed to politics and power—was the right way to go, yet reason is the thought that the universe is knowable and rational and myth is the thought that the universe contains great mysteries that can never be fully known. Can both of these be true? If so, how?

I am diverging from the direction Campbell took, but reason and myth both point to a Creator that exists in reality as well as mythically. God is able to be known and at the same time can never be fully known. Reason and myth are the qualities of faith. For this reason we use the tools at our disposal, like Luke used the X-wing starfighter and its weapons to attack the Death Star in *Episode IV: A New Hope*, and yet just like Luke, we also must let go to a large degree and not only ask for God's help but also allow him to help.

There was a real, actual and historical man called Jesus, who was crucified. This much we know from many more sources than the Bible. And yet, we do not really know if he was the Messiah. It takes faith. It also takes faith to believe that Jesus will come back again, and the Bible tells us about how it will be when he does. This longing for a savior we've never seen and yet know is why myth is so real to us.

Finally, it is through reason and myth we can understand that we must actively pursue selflessness and truth both individually and as a society. These are the only ways we can maintain the longevity of a healthy and free civilization. The question is, how can we reach these lofty goals with the mess we make of things? **Star Wars Jesus** is the answer. We have to look to him.

CONCLUSION
THE PERSISTENCE OF MYTH

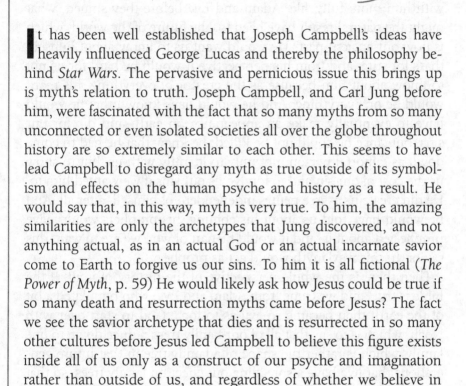

It has been well established that Joseph Campbell's ideas have heavily influenced George Lucas and thereby the philosophy behind *Star Wars*. The pervasive and pernicious issue this brings up is myth's relation to truth. Joseph Campbell, and Carl Jung before him, were fascinated with the fact that so many myths from so many unconnected or even isolated societies all over the globe throughout history are so extremely similar to each other. This seems to have lead Campbell to disregard any myth as true outside of its symbolism and effects on the human psyche and history as a result. He would say that, in this way, myth is very true. To him, the amazing similarities are only the archetypes that Jung discovered, and not anything actual, as in an actual God or an actual incarnate savior come to Earth to forgive us our sins. To him it is all fictional (*The Power of Myth*, p. 59) He would likely ask how Jesus could be true if so many death and resurrection myths came before Jesus? The fact we see the savior archetype that dies and is resurrected in so many other cultures before Jesus led Campbell to believe this figure exists inside all of us only as a construct of our psyche and imagination rather than outside of us, and regardless of whether we believe in him or not.

What are we to make of this? Do we concede that Jesus is just another copy of the savior archetype in myth, and so, sooner or later, society was bound to make him up on the grand scale we now have him?

Perhaps. As stated many times before, there is no proof for Jesus, God incarnate . . . we'd hardly need faith if there were. But let us suppose, just for a minute, that God is real, that a holy and loving and creative God does exist, and that he made and set this whole universe in motion, that he is omniscient and omnipotent and all things good and superlative.

If God made us, and right from the start made himself known to us, as in there really was an Adam and an Eve that God came and hung out with in the evening (Genesis 2 and 3), and they sinned and he, God, wanted to restore our relationship so we could hang out with him more fully, like Adam and Eve before they sinned, what might the natural result have been for the future of the world, which is now our ancient past? He would want us to know about himself, that's for sure, and from his perspective it would be hard for us not to know about him because as the creator of everything, his mark would be on everything. And he would have known that he would have to eventually make an appearance on earth and die for our sins, but since he could not be killed, he knew that he had to come down as a mortal person, not only to identify with us, but to show us the cost of our sin and to forgive us our sins if we wanted him to. He did create us as free beings independent of himself, after all. And he would have told us about his coming, his prophets would have prophesied about it, and it would be part of who we are to want this savior. In this way, myth would act as prophesy.

Then there is the whole perspective of the history of it all. If the Bible is true, and we came from Adam and Eve, who populated a bit of the earth then became so evil as to force God to start over with Noah, which is to say that all of our family trees reduce down to one family, which is rather the shape of a family tree in that future generations that live have a spreading out effect on family trees, so that going backwards might very well reduce back to one family, then how scary is that!. So if this is true you can see where this is leading. The cultures that from one perspective in time do not seem to have any commonality of background, or came to find themselves in isolated communities, would have further back in time have come from somewhere common and as such had similar stories. And just as you cannot play telephone without the end person getting a distorted message, the actual telling and relaying of the myth would get distorted over time and place and different parts of the story would get exaggerated depending on what was going on with that people group.

If God made the human race, we would also share great commonality of form and being amongst all of us. So the psychological, myth-creating impulses that we all have, in different times and in different places would, by nature, leak out part of who God has shown himself to be to us, and natural expressions would come out in our unconscious dreams and the biography of our personal lives, as Freud found, and in the unconscious biology of our humanity, as Jung found.

Myth coming about through this reasoning is much more logical and cohesive than simply believing in the random origin of myths. This position takes none of the wonder and none of the mystery out of myth. If anything, it increases and gives scope to the amazing testament of our present oneness with ancient isolated cultures and God's persistent and unified calling to all of his people, so that when everyone is finally able to read the Bible in his or her own language they can understand that they are being reunited with their ancient past and with their true Creator. In this sense, myths are like John the Baptist, shouting to us to make way for Jesus, the real savior archetype who actually lives. This would mean that believing in Jesus would involve believing in the myth that not only came true, but is true and has been true since before man. Jesus would then be the creator of myth, and the myths of man would then be using his image, the power he gave us, to create . . . just like he does.

ABOUT THE AUTHOR

Caleb Grimes' faith journey has paralleled the films in many ways, and as such is inextricably linked to them. He came to Christ the same month Star Wars (*A New Hope*) was released to theaters—his family saw it at a drive-in in southern California. Caleb's "Dagobah experiences," that of having Christian masters teach him, occurred in the study centers, books and seminars of L'Abri (started by Francis Schaeffer), then in two years at Wheaton College. He attends churches that have balanced the mind of Christ (good theology) with the "flowing" of the Holy Spirit (charisma)—which is very much the well-rounded nature of Star Wars spirituality. He met his wife because of their mutual love of seeing Jesus in Star Wars. Ironically, they fell in love and were married in 2001, the same year that Episode II came out, in which Anakin and Padme fell in love and were married! Finally, in 2005, Caleb and family decided to escape "the Empire" (DC Metro area) and pursue his writing career and his wife's painting career by moving to a remote town in Virginia; very similar to Obi-Wan's exile at the end of Episode III, which came out that same year.

As part of generation X, Caleb Grimes comes from the perspective of pop culture being a natural part of his life, and something in which the good and bad mix together as part of a post-Christian environment. Instead of being daunted by this, he is invigorated and sees opportunities to rightly understand the value and the pitfalls in the philosophies present in movies, songs, books . . . and of course Star Wars in particular. Because his life has always had one foot in the Christian world and one in the "outside" world he has always been involved with church, but never solely defined by it. In a similar vein, he loves Star Wars, but is not possessed by it. Caleb Grimes is primarily a fiction writer, so he views Christian apologetics through the truth of stories instead of philosophy and theology by themselves. For him, then, learning about a life of faith is to visualize it through the metaphors of Star Wars.

He wrote an ariticle for Hollywoodjesus.com on this subject that was published the same day that *Episode II—Attack of the Clones* was released to theaters in 2001. He has written short stories and is writing a novel, none of which he has yet tried to publish.

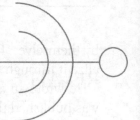

BIBLIOGRAPHY

1. *The Power of Myth*, Joseph Campbell and Bill Moyers, p. 206, Anchor Books, 1991
2. *The Quotable Lewis*, # 868/The Weight of Glory (chap. 1, para. 11–12, pp. 15–16), C.S. Lewis, Tyndale, 1989
3. *The Quotable Lewis*, # 875/Surprised by Joy (chap. 5, para 10, p. 78), C.S. Lewis, Tyndale, 1989
4. *Mystery and Manners*, "The Grotesque in Southern Fiction," Flannery O'Connor, Farrar, Straus and Giroux, 1969
5. *The Mind of the Maker*, Dorothy Sayers, Harper Collins, 1941
6. *The Quotable Lewis*, # 1493/*God in the Dock*, "Myth became Fact," Wayne Martindale, Jerry Root editors, Tyndale, 1989
7. *Skywalking*, Dale Pollock, Da Capo Press, 1999
8. *Star Wars and Philosophy, The Far East of Star Wars*, Walter (Ritoku) Robinson, Kevin S. Decker, Jason T. Eberl editors, Open Court, 2005
9. *The Power of Myth*, Joseph Campbell and Bill Moyers, p. 5, Anchor Books, 1991
10. *The Power of Myth*, Joseph Campbell and Bill Moyers, p. 33, Anchor Books, 1991
11. *The Power of Myth*, Joseph Campbell and Bill Moyers, p. 33, Anchor Books, 1991

RELATED BOOKS

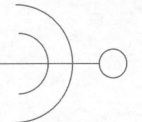

The Tao of Star Wars, John M. Porter, M.D., Humanics, 2003

The Dharma of Star Wars, Matthew Bortolin, Wisdom, 2005

*The Journey of Luke Skywalker—An Analysis of Modern Myth and Symbol, Steven A. Galipeau, Open Court, 2001

Using the Force, Will Brooker, Continuum, 2002

Star Wars: The New Myth, Michael J. Hanson and Max S. Kay, Xlibris, 2001

The Hero With A Thousand Faces, Joseph Campbell, Princeton University Press, 1949

Prayer—Finding the Heart's True Home, Richard J. Foster, Harper Collins, 1992

Unlocking the Mystery of the Force, Frank Allnut, Allnut Publishing, 1983

---

*Highly recommended

RELATED BOOKS

To order additional copies of this title call:
1-877-421-READ (7323)
or please visit our web site at
www.winepressbooks.com

If you enjoyed this quality custom published book,

drop by our web site for more books and information.

www.winepressgroup.com

"Your partner in custom publishing."